P9-BYO-211

"Fr. Ike has taken women from the fringes of New Testament events and has given them voice. Through them he has made very personal our deepest concerns. The women come alive as they speak of the brokenness we all share. We rejoice with them as we hear how their lives changed once they met Jesus. We are challenged to imitate them....

"Read the last chapter first. 'The Grandmother' most truly presents the Fr. Ike who continues to tell of God's compassion, care, and concern for us—and who once again encourages us, with that love to love one another."

Velma McDonough, LCSW
Clinical Psychotherapist
Author of *Mary Remembers*

"The New Testament, a product of a male-run church, illustrates amply the contributions of men to the birth and growth and eventual life of the church. On the other hand, we must train ourselves to savor the gospels' and Acts' subtle clues testifying to the wonderfully varied and vital ways in which women have also lived Jesus' ministry. *Women of the Gospel* is a good place to start. Fr. Ike sets some of those stories in conversation with sound scriptural exegesis, showing us how to savor clues so subtle that we can easily overlook them. He helps us to observe women doing Christ's work in the most impossible of situations. His stories of women of the gospel should help to change us all for the better. We need this book."

Dr. Philip J. McBrien
Author, *How to Teach with the Lectionary* and
Exploring the Sunday Readings

"For once the silent women of the gospel speak out. Haven't you ever wanted to sneak up on them—Peter's mother-in-law, or the future mother-in-law at the marriage of Cana, or the sinful woman who washed Jesus' feet—and shout: 'Speak! Don't just stand there! Tell me what you are thinking'? Each of these women speaks to something—or someone—within ourselves: we all have our shy self, our left-out self, our embarrassed self, our sinful self.

"Each of us, whether man or woman, married or single, in-laws and out-laws, feel a bond with these women of the gospel, due to the perceptive sensitivity of Father Isaias."

Carroll Stuhlmueller, C.P.
Catholic Theological Union

"Isaias Powers clearly has compassion for the human situation, a sense of people's grandeur in the midst of faltering and foibles. He also has a flair for speaking what comes through in Scripture as 'the mind of Christ.' The fact that the voices of *women* are used to elaborate on the behind-the-scenes aspects of gospel moments adds greatly to the book's interest.

"A fine storyteller, Powers offers a rich resource for the reader's prayerful imagination. Every story and every character comes to life with a practical, spiritual lesson for today. Foremost among these lessons is Powers' convincing portrayal of the way in which God is present and continually giving gifts in the nitty-gritty of human ordinariness. The author is to be applauded for his ability to proclaim the 'good news' in multiple voices that cross the centuries. He is to be congratulated too for the special empathy he shows for the weak and the weary, the woebegone and downtrodden, as well as the 'somebodies' who bear the weight of others' high expectations. *Women of the Gospel* succeeds in showing—in a very contemporary way—how all of these types (represented by 28 women) together create caring Christian community and testify to the life of God-with-us."

Pamela Smith, SS.C.M.
Author, *WomanStory: Biblical Models for Our Times*

ISAIAS POWERS

Illustrated by Betty Iovine

WOMEN
OF THE GOSPEL

Sharing God's Compassion

TWENTY-THIRD PUBLICATIONS
Mystic, Connecticut 06355

Second printing 1993

Twenty-Third Publications
185 Willow Street
P.O. Box 180
Mystic CT 06355
(203) 536-2611
800-321-0411

© Copyright 1993 Isaias Powers. All rights reserved. No part of this publication may be reproduced in any manner without prior written permission of the publisher. Write to Permissions Editor.

ISBN 0-89622-521-6
Library of Congress Catalog Card Number 92-81796

PREFACE

Any similarity between these 28 gospel women and the people living today is meant to be more than coincidental. Both in and out of the confessional, for over 30 years, I have listened to people—the outside of what they said, and the inside too. I have identified certain moods, feelings, customary ways of reacting to life's situations (the good as well as the bad side of each) and I have given them names. They are the gospel women in this book.

These stories did not begin with the gospel; they began with the people I listened to. As I thought of them, I wondered how many people could identify with the women our Lord had befriended while on earth. Then I thought how naturally these friends of Jesus could be conduits of God's compassion for us today. All they need is the opportunity to speak up.

Thus these pages.

CONTENTS

WOMEN
OF THE GOSPEL

Introduction

I am an advocate of right thinking about God, round-the-clock right thinking. The better we understand the loving and compassionate nature of God the Father, the more good we will find in ourselves and others. Most people say "Amen" and "Oh yes!" when they sing about God as love and when they hear psalms and gospel passages about the tenderheartedness of the Lord of Abraham, Isaac, Jacob, and Jesus. But this concept—what one might call the kindly aspect of the deity—is usually reserved for church, prayer times, and a few other special occasions.

At other times, however, God is more likely to be imagined as having a sterner countenance. The following quotation from the *Chicago Tribune* a few years ago sums up the most telling characteristics of how ordinary people, *ordinarily*, think about how God relates to people:

> Elia Kazan, a Hollywood director of note for many years, describes his job: "The director of movies no longer exists to flatter artists. Films are no longer made solely to show off actors. Those Hollywood days are over....And what makes a good director? Directors should act like God," he said, *"aloof, judgmental, demanding and, at times, severe."*

It is too bad Mr. Kazan thinks like that. But that is certainly the ordinary way most people think of God. Do you remember the last time you heard somebody say:

> "He thinks he's God!"
> "She goes around acting like God!"
> "The way they strut about, you'd think they were God!"

Do these statements suggest any kindly attributes? Or are they criticisms based on attributes similar to what Mr. Kazan thinks God is: aloof, judgmental, demanding and, at times, severe?

Once! Just once, I'd like to hear God mentioned with more tender and merciful attributes! Just once, I'd like to hear a statement like these:

"He is so forgiving and patient, he reminds me of God!"
"She is so kind and compassionate and helpful, she is like God!"
"That couple is so creative and delighted with life, they act like God!"

Only Jesus knows who God is. And he told us and showed us all about it. With parables and direct statements, he taught us what his Father is like. He also healed many people and performed other kindly deeds of love, linking these acts of compassion to the words, "If you have seen me, you have seen my Father, also."

In order to promote "right thinking" about God, I therefore present in this volume 28 gospel women who tell us their experiences of Jesus'—and therefore his Father's—loving compassion. Remember, the 28 gospel women in this book are, *at this moment*, volunteering to help you be comforted by these considerations.

I hope you will enjoy reading about these gospel women as much as I have enjoyed writing about them.

Setting the Scene

The time is now. The place, an ampitheater in heaven. All the angels and saints are assembled according to divine classification of respect and dignity. The throne of God is decked out like an office of a chief executive officer in a very efficient enterprise. At the large desk is God the Father, Jesus, and his mother, with the apostles fanning out on either side. A number of women sit in straight chairs, close by. On one side there is a podium where each will soon speak.

Although countless people are assembled, everyone has a good view (one of the advantages of heaven). Also, nobody misses a word, because the acoustics are perfect. Everything is perfect.

God Speaks

I have called this committee meeting to find new ways to expedite matters of compassion. There are a lot of troubled and perplexed people on earth. Many of them seldom think of coming to me with their problems. I'm considered the "bad guy": aloof, judgmental, superior, often even scarey.

I want this emphasis to change. My main purpose for sending Jesus to earth was to present me as I really am: warm and kindly. That is why I have appointed this new commission, headed by the Twenty-Eight, all women, carefully chosen to fill these newly-created cabinet posts. I want them all to be women because they will more readily bring out the maternal side of my nature. Also, I have decided that these women should be connected to the gospel setting, living and struggling with their problems during the gospel years. They will be able to speak of Christ's kindly ways with people because they have experienced this firsthand during their time on earth.

Most of these women are not very well known. That's good; the apostles and the other favorite saints, after all, have enough to do; their phones are always busy with petitions. I want people who are free to deal with this ministry.

It is my wish that each member of this committee concentrate on those who are *not* praying...or don't even realize that we want them to turn to us. The committee members will do research and seek out those who are in need, and then direct them to our attention and loving care.

From our preliminary meetings, all of you Twenty-Eight have a general idea of what I want. Each of you has a particular area of concern. You will specialize in those who need your unique compassion. Make sure your Care People realize that they can identify with you. You see, the most natural and spontaneous thing is to seek help from someone who can understand what's going on...because she "has been there." Nothing quite beats experience to bring out genuine compassion.

Of course, there will be some overlapping of responsibilities. It may happen that some of the Care People of one woman will be the Care People of another, as well. That's all right. You are not competing with each other. You are helping me bring a rich bounty of loving kindness to a world that is already beginning to grow sterile with indifference.

I know whom I have already chosen for this new commission. And I know why. But I want to hear you articulate your mission statement—your goals and hopes—so that all heaven will hear you volunteer and be able to back you up in whatever ways you wish.

Of course, my Son will have the last word and ratify your appointments. Let us begin...

1 Worrying About What People Will Think

Mrs. What

MOTHER OF THE BRIDE AT CANA

There was a wedding at Cana of Galilee, and the mother of Jesus was there. Jesus and his disciples had likewise been invited to the celebration. At a certain  point, the wine ran out and Jesus' mother told him, "They have no wine." Jesus replied, "Woman, how does this concern of yours involve me? My hour has not yet come." His mother instructed the servants, "Do whatever he tells you."

[Jesus then changed 150 gallons of water into the choicest wine....] Jesus performed this first of his signs in Cana of Galilee. Thus did he reveal his glory, and his disciples believed in him.

John 2:1-11

Mrs. What Speaks

Please, Father, let me speak first. I was right there during the very first of Christ's signs. Somebody has to start this. Let it be me.

You all know my name. But let the people on earth know me as "Mrs. What," which stands for "What will people think of me?" That was the big problem I had at the wedding reception in Cana, way back then. My daughter, too: same problem. She was such a lovely bride. We were both bothered to a frenzy about the sudden shortage of wine. "What will my family and friends think of us, not being able to show hospitality at such an important occasion?" This concern became an almost total preoccupation.

Oh, my husband was worried, too. So was the groom. But we two were devastated. We always placed so much importance on other people's opinions of us. We would have been disgraced if our friends became disdainful because they thought we were stingy or discourteous, not living up to the expectations of the event.

That's the way we felt, the afternoon in question. We were mortified—sick at heart—embarrassed no end! It wasn't my husband's fault. He had prepared plenty of food and drink for the 40 or so guests. Actually, it was Jesus' fault. Everybody here knows this. Yes, I see him smiling. I can enjoy it too...*now*. But at the time, it was most unsettling.

How did we know that Jesus would bring six of his disciples at the last minute? The "thirsty six" I called them: Peter and Andrew, James and John, Philip and Nathaniel. Our provisions plummeted as soon as they came in. The wine ran short the quickest! Everything was headed for disaster. We would have to apologize, cut short the celebration, then run off and hide. For many years after, I would go to market and wince, because I would feel people whispering about me behind my back: "They were too cheap to care for the bride and groom on their big day! They disgraced the rules of hospitality and themselves!"

I just wanted to cry. But I looked over at Mary. She was so calm. And to think of it, she should have been more upset than I. Her own son publicly refused to do her a favor! It was a natural request on her part. I'm sure she thought Jesus would have sent a couple of his disciples back to town or to their own homes to bring more wine. But he refused her simple request. And there were some very strange words he said—he called his own mother "Woman"—and he referred to a very mysterious "hour."

Everybody stopped talking. Nobody dared miss what was coming next. Then the miracle was performed: over 150 gallons of the best wine we ever enjoyed, any place! Joy turned aside all my anxiety. Jesus called what he did a sign—the first one—to show that the goodness of God is *much more than we could hope for.*

Of course, I quickly understood the purpose for that apparent quarrel between mother and son. Jesus had to get everybody's attention. He did not want his disciples to miss the meaning of the compassionate cordiality of our God.

Well, as you know, from that day on, I have not been so sensitive about what other people think of me. I just did what I could...and refused to fret over what I could not change. If people threatened me with silence or contempt, or if I didn't come up to their standards, too bad about them! I determined not to live according to whether other people approved or disapproved of me. Jesus showed me how much more important it is for God to approve of me. I finally grasped the fact that, if God said I was okay, I was okay...no matter how many others gave me thumbs down.

And here I am. My husband and I finally made it to this "thumbs up" place, here, where we now know a joy our little back-yard party at Cana only hinted at.

Therefore, good Father, I want to care for those people still on earth who are a lot like me. Men and women both. People my age, and especially young people my daughter's age. There is a tremendous force of peer pressure going around. Many youth get hooked on drugs or drink because of it. Some are crushed and sulk for weeks if they can't keep up the pace with their friends, or if their parents won't let them go to the big parties or wear the "right" clothes. They feel like their world has ended.

And some adults will do *anything* not to offend a group they want to belong to. Others, to make sure they "belong," will join in the most malicious gossip or take part in the most offensive kinds of bigotry and bias. Yes, and there are professional people who allow injustices because if they don't they will be blackballed from the "in group."

Also, Father, a lot of individuals refuse to trust you, or to confess their sins, because they think you are so disappointed with them that you have banned them from your society. They are so ashamed when somebody catches them in sin or discovers some other mistake they made. They can't stand themselves, and then they think that *you* can't stand them, either.

Please, Father, let me help persuade them that you deal with them much more kindly than they deal with themselves. You love them. You won't sentence them to silence or contempt. If they will only let me reach them, I will help them live more happily, not worried so much about what others think and not so depressed about their past faults and wrongdoings.

So, Father, I volunteer to concentrate my energies and your compassion on those people who are oversensitive about human opinions, and those who are so ashamed of their past that they don't have much hope left. I will boost their hope; and, with your grace, they will make it all the way to our lovely "thumbs up" world.

Jesus Speaks
Father, I ratify Mrs. What for this assignment. She will be good. She has a maternal heart. At Cana, she cared so much for her daughter. She wanted everything to go well. She knows—you might say she knows *by heart*—how to understand those people who very much want things to go well. And she knows from experience what strong feelings erupt when things don't go well. She can help those people to consider *our* criterion about what is pleasing, instead of fearing the world's standards about such things. She can offer hope to those who feel outside the group's approval.

It will be good for everyone to know that people should pray to us when a big crisis comes up, but we are just as compassionate about little problems, too. Little problems, as we all know, never seem little at the time. The worst that could have happened at Cana is that a few people would have suffered embarrassment because of a lack of hospitality. An outsider may call such a problem no big deal, but it was to them. And we want to help, to offer our care and compassion for all our creatures, in whatever situation they are in. This was part of the sign I worked at Cana; I wanted all to trust our kindliness.

God Speaks

So be it. Good. We are launched into our new work, thanks to the gracious volunteering and the good insights of Mrs. What.

One further idea. I want to expand my concern for those who are troubled by "What will people think of me?" to include all those who are so poor or sick or disfigured and handicapped that they cannot even consider having a party in their back yard. They don't even get so far as to worry about the possibility that they might be shamed; they *start* with the stigma of society's put-downs.

My Son, I want you to put your best people on this job. Let my compassion be felt by those too poor to celebrate anything, too sick to enjoy anything, or too disabled to feel genuinely included in anybody's joy...that is, in anybody's joy but ours.

Citizens of heaven, what do you say?

They all respond, "Amen."

THE STORY OF

Mrs. Left Out

ST. PETER'S MOTHER-IN-LAW

[After the call of Peter and Andrew, James and John] Jesus entered Simon Peter's house. Now Simon's mother-in-law  was suffering from a great fever and they all besought Jesus for her. And standing over her, he rebuked the fever and it left her. and [then] she rose at once and began to wait on them.

Matthew 8:14; Mark 1:29

Mrs. Left Out Speaks

God, Father, I would like to be next to volunteer. Jesus performed his second miracle for me. And my concerns—my "expertise" in the realm of feelings—are very close to those of Mrs. What.

In her experience and mine, Jesus cared for ordinary people, whose concerns were ordinary setbacks. At Cana, it was not a matter of life or death, but possible embarrassment caused by inadequate hospitality. In my case, I only had a little fever. I might have been a week in bed and then I'd be up again. But I would have missed out on the party and have been so miserable, hearing all the excitement downstairs and not being able to join in.

As you know, Father, your Son is always so considerate of people's feelings. When Peter and Andrew, then James and John, left their fishing nets, they determined to join the Lord on the spot. But they didn't just leave without a goodbye. Jesus saw to that.

There was a big send-off. We all needed to take some time with our farewells. It was important to have those last moments of tenderness and love...and words of caution about taking warm clothes...and a chance for parents and in-laws and wives and children to have those last hugs and words to remember. Our sense of loneliness would have been too much to bear unless we all joined in and celebrated their leave-taking.

But I was upstairs, hearing about all this secondhand. It was awful! I was always convinced that I wasn't very important. Nobody cared very much about me. The only exciting thing about my life was my two daughters. Now they are all grown up and married...and their husbands are going off with Jesus, and I'm not even there to give them any instructions. Something really special was going on inside my own house, and I felt so left out!

I was beginning to wallow in self-pity. I even feared I would soon die from my fever—I even wanted to—when suddenly the door opened. In came Jesus, the mother of James and John leading the way. Then, as easily as he lifted up my hand, he commanded the fever to leave my body. And it did, just like that! It felt wonderful; it was so exciting. I jumped out of bed, hugged the Lord, laughing all the time. Then I went into the bathroom, dried my tears of joy, put on my work clothes, and ran to the kitchen to help out...and to catch up on all the news I missed.

Toward the end of that lovely evening, Jesus gathered all of us, all but the little children, and told us why the disciples had to leave home and go with him. He was wonderful, the way he explained it. He was the promise we were all praying for...all our lives. The sacrifice of our sons and husbands was for a good cause; it was for love and a preparation for the life that we enjoy right now. But as joyful as our world of heaven is, I'll never forget the happiness and the heart-felt hope that evening when Jesus cured my fever and I said goodbye to my dear son-in-law.

So I want to volunteer as a special agent of your compassion, Father, for those men and women who are bored to death in their sickbeds. Some are seriously ill, some are old, and both know they will die soon. Others have fevers like mine; still others are laid up because of accidents or other illnesses. Their condition does not have the fear of death in it, but they suffer just the same. Medical expenses are mounting, they cannot work, and they are missing many of life's joys and undertakings. They feel left out, the way I did.

Let me comfort them with your compassion, Father. I'll know how to reach them, if only they'll let me do so. I'll know what to say to encourage them, because I suffered in the same way. I'll point out two good prospects to give them hope, despite their fears and loneliness.

The first possibility is a sudden cure. Perhaps Jesus will take pity on their plight and heal them as he commanded my fever to leave me. Once they recover, they'll be better at visiting the sick because they'll know what it means to be bedridden.

If the healing doesn't happen—and for most, this will be the case—I will help them activate their faith in you. I'll turn their thoughts from concentrating on themselves to thoughts of you and the teaching of your Son: why Jesus went to all that trouble to gather disciples, promise heaven in so many parables, then die on the cross and rise again so that all his words would have the ring of truth to them.

And they'll learn to hope again, and wait with patience for the time when Jesus will take them home, to be with us where every tear is washed away and loneliness and boredom are nothing but a memory.

Jesus Speaks

Good Father, I ratify the selection of Simon Peter's mother-in-law. Let her be called "Mrs. Left Out" for this commission. She has always been a delightful person, full of joy and encouragement. Peter will agree; they always got along so well. After I healed her, she went about soothing the worries that troubled her daughter and the other wives. She made it much easier for them to let their husbands go. She will be good at relieving the fears of those who must soon let go of their own lives and greet death...and wait for my hand to raise them up to our world here.

Also, she will be a good maternal presence to all who languish in sickbeds, wishing they weren't so bored and lonely. Hope and compassion emanate from her. She has all the right instincts for the sickbed situations. Let her begin her mission.

God Speaks
So be it. Care for them well, Mrs. Left Out, and care also for the homeless who can't afford a sickbed. Because of their poverty, they feel left out of everything. Remind them of my compassion and love. And do what you can to influence the world's powerful ones to alleviate the plight of the destitute and others who despair.

You have a full work load. Begin. I will be with you.

The citizens of heaven respond, "So will we all. Amen."

3 When You Feel Rejected

Mrs. Put Out

THE SAMARITAN WOMAN

Jesus, wearied as he was from the journey, was sitting at the well....There came a Samaritan woman to draw water.... [She] said to Jesus, "How is it that you, a Jew, ask for a drink of water from me, a Samaritan woman? [Jews do not associate with Samaritans.] Jesus said, "Go, call your husband and come back." The woman said, "I have no husband." Jesus said to her, "You have spoken truly....You have had five husbands and the man you now have is not your husband...." The woman left her water jar and went back to town and said to the people, "Come and see a man who has told me all that I have ever done."...Many in that town believed in Jesus because of the word of the woman who bore witness....But they said to the woman, "We no longer believe because of what you have said, for we have heard for ourselves...!"   John 4:1-54

Mrs. Put Out Speaks

Good Father, the Care People of Mrs. What are those who fear group pressure, anxious that they might be embarrassed in front of their friends. They are afraid: "What will people think if I do this or that." The Care People of Mrs. Left Out are those who, through nobody's fault, become sick and old, and so they can't take part in ordinary joys and pastimes.

My Care People will be those who are already put out of other people's lives. They are the shunned, the ostracized, those rejected by a group or society, the nobodies of everybody else's world. That was my case, all right! Even after my association with Jesus, I was still considered a person of no consequence by those snobs in Samaria.

Oh, it was my fault, to a certain extent; I'm not denying that. We Samaritans had the Ten Commandments, too. And I broke them. I was going to make amends. I had already decided to leave my man and return to my real husband; that is, I was on the point of doing so. Jesus prodded me to put my idea into action.

My problem was that I was too attractive for my own good. Because of my beauty, I was always flirting. It was mostly a game. In fact, that was what I was doing at the well. I was trying to flirt with the stranger from Galilee...just to see what would happen.

Oh, it "happened" all right. Christ's words completely smashed my veneer of sophistication, which was my protection, and told me what I knew all along but would not admit. So I confessed my sins and promised amendment; I felt the peace of his compassion and forgiveness. It was wonderful.

Then a change took place in my attitude toward the townspeople. The feeling of being forgiven can alter a lifestyle that's been building up for years. As you know, Father, my neighbors wouldn't speak to me. They hated me intensely. They called me whore and many other terrible things. The women were jealous of my beauty; the men were afraid of my charm. They worried about the bad example I gave the children. So they had nothing to do with me, and I had nothing to do with them. I hated their snobbery and self-righteous airs. I had my tricks, my ways to get even. I'm ashamed of these, too.

Well, when Jesus forgave me, I didn't nurse my grudge any longer. I was so filled with love, Father, as Jesus gave it to me, that I went to tell the townspeople all about what the Lord had said and done to me. They were amazed that I spoke to them at all, but my enthusiasm and my real honesty amazed them even more. They didn't like me or trust me, but they saw such a change in me that they had to investigate.

The whole world knows what happened after that; it's in the gospel. The people still refused to warm up to me. Even after Jesus talked to them and changed their lives, they couldn't resist taking a final shot at an old enemy. I can still feel the venom in their words: "We now believe, but not because of you (you nobody!); we believe because we heard it ourselves!"

Well, too bad about them! I left soon after...with my real husband and we went to Tyre where we lived well enough. We lived the fullness of the Holy Spirit after Barnabas baptized us and our children. We died with grace as our companion. And now we live—forever, happily—with you.

So Mrs. Put Out is my name for this commission. And I would like to show divine compassion on all those who feel pushed aside in any way. My talent for flirting has turned into a virtue; I can still be appealing, and that's a good thing: to make the fruits of forgiveness and the consequences of God's love a most appealing advantage.

Everybody feels cast off, one way or another. Boy has jilted girl. Girl has jilted boy. Friend has deceived friend. Certain members of a family have mocked family loyalty by their wayward lives. Groups of workers sometimes ban a fellow worker from all practical association. Racial bias—all forms of bigotry—makes people feel driven apart. Sheltered positions in politics, religion, and other professions are so preciously protected that outsiders fear to cross the line. Individuals— from kindergarten to nursing homes—can feel that they are banned from society. Parents are neglected because their children don't communicate with them or visit them. Children run away from home because they feel their parents don't care about them. My guess is that everybody feels put down by somebody, sometime.

I'll help them, Father, as much as I can. I know what it's like to be put down by friends and neighbors. It still hurts when I think of how I suffered from silent contempt and cruel taunts. I'll help them let go of some of their bitterness. If they'll only give me half a chance, I'll draw them into your compassion and give them such an experience of your loving kindness that they'll never forget it; they will never forget you.

Once this happens, they'll feel good about themselves, as I did. They'll be so relieved, and so busy helping others, they won't have time to fret over the ones who don't accept them.

Time is running out. I want to get to them before they give up altogether. Please give me leave to be your minister of mercy.

Jesus Speaks

Yes, by all means, give my Samaritan friend the assignment. She speaks very well; her conversations are always going someplace. She has the knack of cheering people up. They may be feeling so dismal they don't want her company, as in Samaria, but she still finds a way to reach them and put hope into their hearts.

I just ask her to take on another task. I'd like her to soften the hearts of the show-offs, the flirts, the pleasers of all kinds. She will mellow them a little, get them to not work so hard to make the "big impression." Once they quit trying so hard and become more genuine, their real goodness will show through. They will be easier to love.

God Speaks

Yes, by all means. Let Mrs. Put Out be so commissioned. And, as she herself has said, there is no time to waste; so many are on the verge of despair.

My Son, our Samaritan friends have much to do. You form a sub-committee of Twelve—six men, six women—to reach the flirts and the pleasers of both sexes.

Notice that this commission will bring compassion and a fresh way of living for all the occupations that depend on other people's good will: politicians, salespeople, entertainers, tour leaders, and so on. Whoever depends on the gift of gab to earn their livelihood, they're the ones I call the "pleasers." When we reach these people, love will counteract all tendencies toward cynicism. Then instead of being moved by the need to control others with their personal appeal, they'll be able to love and kindly serve the people they appeal to.

Let our compassion be the key to this enterprise. In every branch of popularity and unpopularity, our merciful love will broaden the narrow-minded, comfort the hurting, and turn natural virtues, such as glib tongues and good looks, into marvelous new enterprises. What say you all?

The citizens of heaven all say as one, "Amen."

4 Personal Problems You Don't Want to Talk About

THE STORY OF

Shy

THE WOMAN AFFLICTED WITH HEMORRHAGING

A great crowd was following Jesus, and pressing upon him. And there was a woman who for 12 years had had a hemorrhage and had suffered much....Hearing about Jesus, she came up behind him in the crowd and touched his cloak. She said, "If I touch his cloak, I shall be saved."

And at once the flow of her blood was dried up...and she was healed of her affliction. Then Jesus, instantly perceiving that power had gone forth from him, turned to the crowd and said, "Who touched my cloak?" The woman, fearing and trembling—knowing what had happened to her—came and fell down before him and told him all the truth. Then Jesus said to her, "Daughter, your faith has saved you. Go in peace and be healed of your affliction."   Mark 5:21-43;
Matthew 9:18ff; Luke 8:40ff

Shy Speaks
Father, I'd like to blurt out what I have to say and get it over with. It's still embarrassing for me to discuss private matters like this, but it's important for people to know that you are always aware of everything about everybody, and that you have compassion for them. And you will, from your compassion, either heal them of their affliction or help them to suffer with greater dignity.

Please, though all the court knows my name full well, I ask that I be known, for my new commission, as Shy—not Ms. or Mrs. Shy—just plain Shy. My Care People are all shy, because of something they don't like to talk about. So was I. That's our connection.

Let me state, straight out, some of the areas of suffering I'll focus on: the women who suffer from menstrual disorders, such as toxic shock syndrome, and from menopause, nervousness, cramps, complications during pregnancy, all those things that may wear down their energy and demoralize them.

Also, I think of the men who are alarmed and depressed: those with prostate problems, or who cannot perform or who have trouble performing the marriage act.

My Care People will also include those who must endure a mastectomy, hysterectomy, or colostomy. I also want to be of service to teenagers and young adults, many of whom suffer from other forms of embarrassment about their bodies. Sometimes a part of their bodies is too small...or too big...or too "flat" or too "busty." Many are so brainwashed by media advertising that they think everybody ought to be the same. They put themselves down by what embarrasses them, and this can become a compulsion in their lives. They don't have the time or energy to devote themselves to anything more important. They're preoccupied with those parts of their body they cannot accept.

It is still somewhat embarrassing for me to speak of such things here in the court of heaven, but it must be done. For so many, these are real problems that affect their emotional and spiritual life, and all they can think about is their own physical problems, real or imagined.

Any one of these things mentioned can be most troublesome, Good Father. In my case, it was a menstrual flow that couldn't be stopped; it was an all-consuming concern. So much time and money was spent on me that I didn't pay much attention to my family. I focused on my own pain and the embarrassment caused by my condition. The neighbors and the poor people I used to help didn't see me much; I stayed out of sight most of the time.

I heard about Jesus, the wonder worker. I wasn't much interested in what he had to say, or in anything else for that matter!

But I hoped he would heal me. I wanted to be sly about it. (Shy and sly go together, as a rule.) My plan was to hide beside a storefront, on a corner. When Jesus passed, I would touch the hem of his cloak. He would be no wiser for it, but power would flow from him and I'd be cured. In my fantasy, I had it all figured out. Then I'd return to my room, where I'd thank God over and over for the miracle. And, in due time, I'd become more active, without anyone noticing the change in me.

Well, as you know, that was not the way it worked out. Jesus healed me in the quiet way I had hoped for, but he didn't let me slink away unnoticed. He called me up, in front of everyone. He wanted me to proclaim in public what I had wanted to keep a secret.

Soon after, I realized why he did this. I had to replace my preoccupations—my lifestyle and my mood-style. I had to let go of that tendency to be all caught up with myself and my own problems. I had to develop an attitude of heart and mind that would let me be grateful to God and publicly admit my need of God, and develop a generosity of spirit that would include others, not just myself.

This, Father, is what I would like to generate in all those who suffer from embarrassing personal disorders such as I had. I want them to know your compassion. I want them to realize that I will intercede for them, asking Jesus to heal their maladies, as he healed mine.

But if the healing does not happen, I want to be with them as they endure their silent suffering. They can talk to me about their fears and pains. I understand. I will help them, if only they'll let me, to get out of their dismal self-centeredness, to be more gentle with themselves. After all, other people depend on them. The world has not ended for them just because they are afflicted; there is much they can still do in many other areas of life.

And finally, I want to be with them during their final hours. This is when they will need compassion most of all. Having suffered for so long, they now face death! Their natural shyness has hindered their ability to hope and trust in God's love, and since this has been going on for so long, they will find it very difficult to imagine any possibility of God's loving mercy. I will open up the future-beyond-the-point-of-death for them.

If they'll give me even the slightest invitation, I'll prepare them for Jesus. He will raise them up to life to be with us in heaven, where he will stop the flow of their fears and long periods of grief as easily as he stopped the flow of my distress.

Father, I ask for this commission. If they will let me help them, I will give them hope. They will finally know compassion.

Jesus Speaks
Good Father, I heartily endorse Shy for this appointment. People who are hurting and embarrassed by delicate physical disorders are very difficult for us to reach because their ailments force them to think only of themselves, and so they cannot hear the hope we hold out for them. Their afflictions, real or perceived, also make them disgusted with themselves; then they think we're disgusted with them, too.

That is why Shy will be so good for them. She suffered the same way; she understands. People can relate to her because she can relate to them. They can have faith in us, because of her. As she experienced your mercy through me, Father, many others will experience our mercy through her. Let her begin her work.

God Speaks
Well said, my Son. I only add more people to Shy's list. Four more categories of the afflicted. I speak of the mentally handicapped, the emotionally unstable, the learning disabled, and those with Alzheimer's disease. These will be difficult to reach, but they need our compassion most of all. I don't want a team of experts to be assigned for these millions of individuals. I want ordinary people who have a lot of patience and compassion, almost as much as mine.

Will I have enough recruits for this assignment? What do you say?

Thousands of inspired citizens of heaven say, "Amen." Then many more who minister to AIDS victims say, "Amen."

5   Developing Faith in Times of Distress

Mrs. Possibility

MOTHER OF JAIRUS'S DAUGHTER

Jesus [with Peter, James and John] came to the house of Jairus, the ruler of the synagogue. And he saw a tumult, people weeping and wailing greatly [over the death of Jairus's daughter]. But Jesus said to them, "Why are you making such a din and weep? The girl is asleep, not dead."

And they laughed him to scorn. But he, putting them all out, took the father and the mother...and entered in where the girl was lying. And taking her by the hand, he said to her, "...Girl, I say to you, arise!" And the girl rose up immediately and began to walk. She was 12 years old...and Jesus directed that something be given her to eat.

Mark 5:21-43; Matthew 9:18ff; Luke 8:40ff

Mrs. Possibility Speaks
God, my Father, I would like to be selected as a special intercessor of your compassion for all those who are grieving over the untimely death of a loved one. I want to direct my energies to parents who have seen their child die...and then to all those who watch helplessly as they see life leave a teenager, crushed by an accident or victim of a disease. I will also care for the families of young soldiers and sailors killed in war; indeed, for all who know how hard it is to get over the grief when young people die. The death of a youth makes death seem even more tragic.

I also want to include everyone who grieves because they miss their loved one: widows and widowers mourning their spouses; children feeling great loss over the death of a parent or grandparent; friends, lovers, business associates... whoever mourns because someone is gone from their lives. Death is always a harbinger of gloom; and very often it is the cause of questioning your goodness, Father, and your compassion.

When confronted by death, people wonder, "How can God be good if God lets my loved one die?" They need some balance to their grief. They must be open to the possibilities of your more extensive and much further-reaching love.

So call me "Mrs. Possibility" for the duration of this assignment. I don't want to be called the "wife of Jairus"; I'd rather be referred to according by my function: I will give people a sense of *possibility* that will nourish their hope when they are grieving.

I think I was the only one who was open to possibility during the awful afternoon of my daughter's wake. Everyone else there, in the living room and on the porch, was sobbing and crying and making a terrible din. And they were scolding you, Father, almost to the point of blasphemy. You were the horrid one, they cried; you were mean and uncaring to let my daughter die so young.

It seemed that their faith meant nothing to them, nothing at all. We all knew that there would be some kind of resurrection. The heroes of the book of Maccabees assured us of that, and we well knew from the book of Job that God gives life and takes it away. Since life is a gift in the first place, how can we fault God when the giver of the gift reclaims it? But these thoughts were, of course, far from the mourners' minds. What triggered their emotions was the injustice of such an untimely death.

Then Jesus arrived with three of his disciples and my husband. They could hardly get into the house. There was such a commotion and boistrous lamentation of flailing arms that nobody noticed them. Jesus told the crowd to quiet down. They looked at him in disbelief. "How dare he interrupt our mourning!" they thought. "We were just getting warmed up, and he's spoiling it!" They didn't think of *possibilities.* Jesus, they knew, was already a famous wonder worker. Some months before this, he had raised up the son of the widow of Naim. There was the chance that he might do the same for my daughter.

My friends and family didn't even think of that, or care what Jesus did for somebody else. They were delirious with grief. Not even the Lord could wedge into their bitterness. When he said, "The girl is asleep, not dead," they jeered at him, shouting him down, not even waiting to hear what he meant.

You remember, don't you, Jesus? That's when you got very angry. I didn't blame you; I was angry, too. I wanted to hear about the possibilities for a miracle, to listen to your words about death, at least. I just waited off to the side.

Then you threw everybody out, and I was so glad you did. Love and mercy cannot work in an atmosphere of unrelenting grief. Once they left, we entered—you and your disciples, my husband and myself. And then it happened, the *sign* of what you would do for everybody, once Easter came: You raised my daughter from her deathbed. And then—I am so glad St. Mark remembered to mention it!—you showed the marvelously practical nature of your thoughtfulness by telling me to get her something to eat.

I want all people to be open to your compassion, Father, and to love the delicate kindness of your dear Son. I would not dare urge those who grieve to stop their mourning; their tears are prayers. They miss their loved ones and should grieve; it's only natural. But they should not mourn as my neighbors did in Galilee. Their faith should put some balance into their bitterness. They must not lose hope. We Christians have other "certainties" than are portrayed in the books of the Hebrew Scriptures; we have our risen Lord to assure us of an everlasting life.

I want to tell my Care People about the full dimension of your love, Good Father. Then they'll grieve for the right reason: because they miss their loved ones, not because their loved ones live no more.

I'll do all I can to bring balance to their sorrow. As Mrs. Possibility, I'll be a good mother for them, and I'll restore their faith in you as the God of life, not death.

Jesus Speaks

Good Father, I ratify, with relish, my good friend from Galilee. And I like the name she chose: Mrs. Possibility. She is very good at compassion, natural compassion. So she'll be very good at being the ambassador of our compassion, too.

I remember that day. It was a very trying afternoon. It really hurt to face such irreconcilable hostility on that porch. She and her husband had the greatest reason to grieve, yet they were the only ones open to my desire to help. They didn't know what I would do, or if I would do anything. Just the same, they allowed me to do as I wished.

And she was gracious afterward. The neighbors were shocked and guilt-ridden when they saw the girl alive again. Mrs. Possibility didn't scold them for their blasphemies or their lack of trust. Instead, she gently eased them back to a better understanding of God's mercy and the truth of the Scriptures.

She will continue to do so for all who grieve over those who have died. Please, Father, appoint her with honor and grant her all the grace and patience she'll need.

God Speaks

Granted. I do so. I only ask one further thing. I also appoint her daughter for a special group of Care People. Let's call her "Teena" for this assignment. She will concentrate on all the teenagers who sometimes experience "little deaths," which, to them, seem very much like the dying she went through when she was 12 years old.

There are so many ways that the lives of young people are crushed: a jilted friendship, exclusion from a group, the lack of understanding from parents or teachers, being teased for having braces, glasses, facial blemishes, athletic clumsiness…many other causes. During such devastating setbacks, they often go into a "coma," as though it were death itself. And they are tempted to quit on life, to take drugs, or to drown themselves in misery by some other means.

Let Teena be sent to help them. She can give them hope. She can touch that part of their hearts that is still untouched by despair. And she can remind them of possibilities for more courage and a sense of their own dignity.

With help from us, they can "come back to life again," as you did, Teena. Try your best to reach them; you speak their language. Your mother will help you. And, of course, my Son and I will be with you all-ways.

And all the saints and angels say, "Amen."

6 Coping With Anger

Mrs. Balance

THE PALESTINIAN WOMAN

Jesus withdrew into the district of Tyre and Sidon. And he entered a house and would not have any one know it; yet he could not be hid. For immediately, a Canaanite (Syrian/ Palestinian) woman from that region came out and cried, "Have mercy on me, O Lord, Son of David; my daughter is severely possessed by a demon." But Jesus did not answer her a word. And his disciples came and begged him, saying, "Send her away, for she is crying after us." But he answered [her request]: "It is not fair to take the children's bread and throw it to the dogs." She said, "Yes, Lord, but even the dogs eat the crumbs that fall from the master's table." Then Jesus answered her, "O woman, great is your faith. Let it be done for you, as you desire." And her daughter was healed at that instant.   Mark 7:24-30; Matthew 15:21-28

Mrs. Balance Speaks

God, my Father, the presentation by Mrs. Possibility—with her plea for balance—urges me to make my presentation now. I will work for balance among all the angry advocates of justice. I would like to balance the righteousness of their causes with the much needed virtues of prudence and a sense of humor.

I was a righteous protestor of all that was wrong in my world. You already know this very well, my Lord. If I lived in the world today, they would be calling me "an activist." There was injustice everywhere and society needed a lot of changing. People were so bigoted; there was discrimination against women, unfair taxes, exploitation of the poor and, of course, there was the terrible hostility between the Palestinians and the Jews.

I was dead set against all this. Even Caesar in Rome must have heard about my shouts for justice, but his soldiers didn't harm me. They wrote me off as powerless. I guess I was powerless, since the only "power" my protests had were against myself. They so overwhelmed me that I ate outrage, slept with it, and could think of nothing else.

Then my daughter became very sick. I thought a demon possessed her, but people today call that malady acute depression. I suppose I was as much to blame as anyone. I spent all my time and energy on righteous causes and protest meetings and, as a consequence, left her alone a lot.

But when she got worse, I became desperate and turned to prayer. Two days after I started praying and devoting more time to the girl, Jesus came to town. The people didn't appreciate him though. As I say, even then, Palestinians hated the Jews, and vice versa. But, I discovered later, Jesus and his disciples planned to rent a seacoast cottage and take a week's vacation, far away from the people who hounded them for miracles. I interrupted their plans. I knew the reputation of the wonder worker from Galilee and—Jew or no Jew—I would not let anything interfere with my daughter's cure. As much as I wanted her cure, I hesitated approaching him; I trembled as I began to plead with the Jew named Jesus.

As you remember, Lord, you responded typically enough. It was one of those centuries-old put-downs of your people. Anyway, that's how it seemed to me when I first heard you say it. I was ready to bristle, as I always did, ready to protest your bigotry. But your eyes caught me up short. You said, "I don't throw morsels to dogs!" But something told me that you were not deriding me (calling me a dog). You seemed to be appealing for another response, something different from the predictable hatred-laden slur that probably would have started another race riot.

I'm not sure why I changed my tactics. The sense of mercy replaced my sense of justice, somehow...and the health of my child was at stake. I didn't think so much of myself or my causes. A wave of faith swept over me. Somehow, I knew Jesus could heal my child, and that he wanted to. I amazed myself and let a little humor creep in. I changed his words into a pun: I smiled at him and turned myself into a puppy asking for crumbs from his table.

You all know the rest of the story. My daughter was healed, and I became the champion of Jesus in my territory. Oh, I never stopped working for social justice. That was—still is—important. But I tempered my protests with prudence. I no longer vented my outrage so strongly that my audience felt degraded by my insults and became defensive. I first entered into their feelings: the causes of their fears and the protectiveness that fostered their bigotry and exploitation. And then with humor I could get them to laugh at their positions that caused unfair treatment of others, and to renounce them. The rest of my presentation shook them up, planting some seeds of doubt in their determination to keep the status quo.

Little by little, I got results. And I was able to devote more time to my family; no longer were they neglected. Then, when Philip the Deacon arrived, I was ready to be baptized. It didn't take long before I assumed a leadership position in the church. My gifts were quickly recognized. I even taught Paul and some others how to approach the Palestinians...and how to put better timing into their preaching. They also needed to learn to be more sensitive to the fears of their audience. If my neighbors were to accept Jesus as their Christ, their lives would be turned all around. My people had to be approached with prudence and balance. Fellow Christians soon gave me the name "Mrs. Balance" because that was characteristic of me.

Because of this characteristic, I volunteer to help all those advocates of justice on earth today. I'd like to set up shop again—just like the old days in Tyre of Sidon—and influence the righteously indignant with a greater capacity for patience, with a feel for the fears and defensiveness that have such a strong hold on people. Treated like this, those people will want to change.

If they'll let me, I'll give those advocates of justice a sense of humor, so that they can laugh at their own quirks that so often come from their own unchallenged seriousness. That sense of humor will help them do what I did: see a sudden change in the mood of others, and turn their bigotry around. My clients, my seekers after justice, can learn in this way to reach the hearts of the unjust.

I know this won't be easy. The righteous, the protesters with an axe to grind, are almost as closed up in their causes as bigots are closed up in their defensiveness. So I will need the help of all the citizens of heaven. Please pray that I can put a wedge of balance into the terrible legacy of bitterness that exists between religions, races, nations, families...and all the different groups that line themselves up as either "haves" or "have nots."

Certainly, this will be difficult. But there are so many people of good will today who are already making advances against injustice and environmental destruction; they will help me. These people and their agencies need a larger sense of your compassion, Father, so that their causes fit the cause of the whole world's happiness.

Please give me permission to begin, Good Father. As I did before, I will just keep plugging away—using my good instincts—and I will get better as I go along.

Jesus Speaks

Yes, Father, let Mrs. Balance have the authority to receive grace for this marvelous adventure; and let her muster all the forces she will need for such a worthy work.

We have to show compassion, even for the bigots and the wicked usurpers of the world's environment...and for the selfish manipulators of human minds and fortunes. We must balance their frenzied ambition with a care for justice and for the rights of earth. We must cure the tendency of the powerful to ride roughshod over other people's needs. We must also find a cure for the fears and bitter memories that one race, and one nation, has against another. The fierce way people hold on to past atrocities is something that has to change... or else our love and compassion will not be understood. We haven't made much headway in this, not in two thousand years. So I ask you, Father, give her your full support.

God Speaks

Indeed I do. And I also ask for the full support of all the saints. Please write down your suggestions and give them to Mrs. Balance to coordinate. When families are feuding, I want one saint from each family to work on this. For embittered nations, races and religions—the Christian/Muslim, Palestinian/Jew, Irish/English, Polish/Russian, black/white, on and on...the saints on each side will work for a healing balance for the other side. I want the saints who were rich on earth to heal the fears of those who are rich today. I want the saints who were poor and downtrodden to give hope, patience, and determination to change things for those who are poor today.

You'd better call a special meeting as soon as possible so that all these plans for action will get under way. Do not get discouraged if you find it slow going; it will take time. I will be with you. Begin.

All the citizens of heaven say, "Amen."

7 Overcoming Shame

Missed Dignity

THE SINNER WHO WASHED JESUS' FEET

Jesus was dining at the house of Simon the Pharisee. And a woman in the town who was a sinner...brought ointment and began to wash his feet with her tears and wiped them with the hair of her head and kissed his feet and anointed them with oil. The Pharisee said [to himself]: "If this man were a prophet, he would know what kind of woman this is—for she is a sinner...." Jesus said, "When I came to your house, you gave me no water for my feet...no kiss...no oil to anoint my head; but she has bathed and kissed my feet...and anointed them with oil. Therefore her sins, her many sins must have been forgiven her, or she would not have shown such great love. It is they who are forgiven little who show little love."
Luke 7:36-50

Missed Dignity Speaks
Mrs. Balance's words about a sense of humor prompts me to

speak next, my God. I had no sense of humor when I was the notorious sinner in town. No sense of gratitude, either—not for God,
not for any human, not for myself. I tried to buy gratitude from
others who bought favors from me. And, of course, I had no sense
of dignity, no appreciation of my own self-worth. Everybody disgusted me as much as I disgusted myself. How can a person who
lives only as a *function* feel like a person?

So it surprised me no end when I was moved with an overwhelming sense of dignity and beauty. I felt it as soon as Jesus arrived on Simon's porch. ("Big Shot Simon" I called him; I knew
him only too well!) Jesus was different from any man I ever met.
He looked at me with love...a love different than any I had ever
come across. He looked at me with *interest*—not sexual or cynical
curiosity—real interest. I was a somebody in his eyes, a mix of
good and bad. He seemed to get right into the good side of me, in-
viting me to bring more of it out.

As I say, it was overwhelming. I know now it was the in-
timation of the perfect happiness of heaven. It was also the start of
my new lifestyle that has gratitude and goodness as its heart. I always had a spirit of generosity. I depended on tips, so I was a big
tipper myself. I also was sensitive to the slights and discourtesy
other people got. Whenever anyone wasn't treated with dis-
respect, I felt it and resented it.

Big Shot Simon slighted Jesus, who was treated with almost the
same disdain I always received. I wanted to give Jesus the courtesy
he deserved. Of course, it was an expensive gesture—the ointment cost almost a week's work—but Jesus was worth it. Because
of the respect he gave me there and then, I felt his gift of peace
come over me.

You all know what came next. Jesus took my generosity and
turned it into gratitude; he took my longing for dignity and
turned it into compunction for my sins; he took my habit of de-
fiance against everyone and changed it to a humble acceptance of
God's love. Then my good side started sprouting out all
over...including my sense of humor, reclaimed at last.

Therefore, Good Father, please call me Missed Dignity, as I volunteer to help the millions of my people still on earth. I certainly

don't want to be known as the "prostitute on the porch." That life-style is long gone. I was thinking of calling myself "Ms. Function" because when I was a sinner of the streets, that's *all* I was, just a function: to please the desires of men; not a real person. But "Missed Dignity" has humor in it; it gets right to the point of what I and all people like me miss the most. People used to use me because I had no dignity, but ever since I met Jesus, that's no longer true. He restored my dignity.

Therefore, I will have more than call girls and children used for pornography as clients. They have first claim on my care, of course. But I also want to bring your compassion, God, to all men and women, young and old, who feel that they are nothing but a *function* in the eyes of others.

I include those housewives who are not really accepted by their family; they are used, not accepted. They face the constant demand that they produce, like a machine: do the cooking, keep the house, drive everybody wherever they have to go...and don't ask questions.

My Care People will also be husbands who are manipulated by their wives, and fathers who are supposed to *function*: as suppliers of money and providers of sports cars...and to "get lost" when it comes to anything personal. I also want to work for the poor: the people on skid row; workers degraded by the lowest forms of employment, workers with no chance for advancement...and for those who receive welfare hand-outs and other forms of government assistance. In all these ways, and many more, the people treated like this feel used, as though they too are prostitutes, only in a different way.

It is their *feelings* I want to get to, Father. I want to be a channel of that same experience and feelings I had when Jesus looked at me, approved my generosity, and then forgave my sins and restored my dignity...and then brought me to all my goodness, stemming from this generosity.

I know these people well, my pleasers. They are sensitive to the plight of others who feel used. Working with their innate goodness and from their own generosity and sympathy for other down-and-outers, I can draw them to a realization of their own self-worth. Once they experience the compassion and forgiveness of your Son, they will "love much," just as the Lord predicted of me, and they will love in the right ways. Their despair and cynicism will turn to gratitude, little by little. They'll reclaim their sense of humor to soften the harshness of a still uncaring world. And they will finally discover that they can make it to our place here, where all put-downs will be put aside, and all their bitter memories will be replaced with lasting joy.

Jesus Speaks

Father, let it be done as she wishes. In all the world—in all its long history—I have met few people as sensitive as Missed Dignity. It was a hot and exhausting day for me, that day in Galilee. No respite...no time even for lunch. My feet were grimy with sand and dirt. I was tired and thirsty. I really looked forward to the nice supper at the house of Simon the Pharisee. According to custom, a servant would wash my feet. My host would then give me clean garments for the feast and I would have a chance to freshen up. But no. I was treated with disdain. I felt I was just a function, too. I was there to defend my activities. The assembled Pharisees wanted me to come only because they wanted to question me (and, they hoped, trip me up) about what I taught and why I healed the infirm without their approval.

I said nothing. I scolded no one. But inside I was hurting. And then my friend (all in Simon's house had called her a sinner), noticing the disappointment in my eyes and the slump of my shoulders, renewed my spirit by refreshing me with her faith, generosity, and expensive ointment.

After she joined our band of disciples, she was always the first at noticing those who felt down in some way. She was so good at cheering them up, reminding them of their dignity and goodness.

She will do the same for all her Care People, if only they give her half a chance. We will be with her, Father. Whenever she is stuck, we'll help her out. I am enthusiastic about her new assignment, because through her we'll be able to help and heal and bring out the best in countless individuals.

God Speaks

Yes, so be it. And remember, Missed Dignity, if you have any questions, we are always available.

One thing more. I have chosen a special group of teenagers and counsellors sympathetic to teenage problems. Many of these young people feel used by their parents; they have to function perfectly, or they are punished. They have to get good grades, or excel on the sports field, or be superior in some way. If they have a bad year or show interest in something different from what their parents had planned for them, they are practically disowned. This is turning people into things-to-be-used, the way prostitution does.

Make sure the subcommittee finds a way to reach them—to love them for themselves. Our compassion wants to give all people integral dignity, not honors based solely on performance.

I need all heaven to sanction me in this. Do I have it?

All the angels and saints respond, "Amen."

8 When You Feel Depressed

The Gloomed One

MARY MAGDALENE

With Jesus [on his journey to Jerusalem] were the Twelve and certain women who had been cured of evil spirits and infirmities. Mary, who is called the Magdelene, from whom seven devils had gone out; Joanna, the wife of Chusa, Herod's steward; Susanna, and many others who used to provide for them out of their means.   Luke 8:2

Now there were standing by the cross of Jesus, his mother and his mother's sister, Mary of Cleopas, and Mary Magdelene.   John 19:25

Now on the first day of the week, Mary Magdelene came early to the tomb, while it was still dark. Mary was weeping at the tomb....Then two angels said to her, "Woman, why are you weeping?" She said to them, "Because they have taken away my Lord and I do not know where they have laid him." ...Then Jesus said to her, "Woman, why are you weeping? Whom do you seek?" She, thinking it was the gardener, said to him, "Sir, if you have removed him, tell me...." Then Jesus said to her, "Mary!" Turning, she said to him, "Master!" Jesus said to her, "Do not touch me...but go to the [others]...."   John 20:1-18

The Gloomed One Speaks

If you please, Father, let me speak next. Since I've often been confused with Missed Dignity who just spoke, I want to show everyone how really unlike we are. We have different problems and for two very different reasons we can help people who need your compassion.

My friend was a prostitute. Because she felt used, she developed a shield for protection. But she continued to ply her trade, giving of herself generously, hoping for some kindness in return. She had an instinctive desire to please others, which was the wedge of goodness that helped Jesus turn her life around.

There was no such wedge in me. When St. Luke finished with the story of Missed Dignity in his gospel, I was introduced. I was one of those "certain women" who followed Jesus and the apostles and were cured of evil spirits. After we were healed, we were so grateful that we volunteered to take care of all the domestic chores at camp. I was the first mentioned among these women. I was connected with the number 7—the "perfect number," as it was considered—the number that said, "You can't get more, or better—or worse!—than this."

That was my case, all right. I couldn't get any worse. In our time, as you know, Father, people were considered "possessed" by the devil if they were depressed or acted strangely and couldn't lead normal lives. This infirmity ranged all the way from being actually possessed by the evil one, to acute melancholia, and then even to a mild form of depression that wouldn't leave.

I suffered from what would be considered today manic depression. The devil of discouragement had pulled me so far down that I couldn't act, or respond to any stimulus. I was deep in a shell and couldn't get out. I put blinders on my life. Just as horses have them by their eyes so that they can see only straight ahead of them, I had blinders on so that I could feel only the pain of my own paralysis.

Then Jesus intruded into my life (at the time, it seemed an intrusion), and I felt his kind eyes and the radiance of his tender compassion right where the only spark of hope in me was still lit. Through him, life started to seep into me, healing the scabs of my despair. I could begin to move about and see people again. I could, at last, accept love and think about loving others.

As you know, Good Father, from then on I devoted myself to putting Christ's goodness to work by helping others out of their sorrows. The apostles themselves were often pulled into depression, especially after Jesus began to tell them that he must suffer and die for sinners. I coated the colic of their despair with reminders that Jesus, who could heal others and restore them to life, would not end his life in a grave. The evil of death and the wicked designs of hatred would not triumph—not ultimately. We could trust Jesus, even when we were very puzzled by his ways of love. I helped the apostles to continue.

And I was with Mary on Good Friday afternoon—a silent comfort for her. My presence was a reminder that Jesus brought me back from a life of acute depression. When I took Mary's arm and led her away from Golgotha, I could sense—even then— her trust in God and the hope she had in the resurrection, despite the anguish in her heart.

Of course, I was never completely cured of my tendency to get depressed. I helped others get out of theirs, but that didn't mean I was not susceptible to it again and again. Once you live in that kind of coma, there is always a pull to return to it. That's the way it was, Easter morning. For two whole days, from Good Friday to early Sunday, I had cheered others up, but then all my hope, all my energy, caved in. Jesus was dead. Nothing had changed. I began to wonder that maybe my whole change of life was a hoax. Nothing was left for me to hope in.

Angels appeared and told me the good news. I did not believe them. I was miserable. All my reasons to continue living died when Christ died. I came to dignify the tomb. What I was cel-ebrating was *my* death. My presence at the grave—a ritual of gloom—was motivated by self-pity.

Then Jesus spoke to me, but tears prevented me from rec-ognizing him. Because of my own crushed hopes, waves of mis-ery completely overwhelmed me. My blinders were on me again. Despair mutilated sight and insight.

Jesus called me by name...my first name...so tenderly, so kind-ly. There was no lecturing, no words of blame for my back-sliding into melancholy. Just "Mary." Then I saw again. Insight came back to me. Confidence returned. He told me to go back to the dis-ciples and help them wait things out. I did. You all know the rest.

Loving God, I have said all this so that we may more fully re-alize how many people in the world are included in my story. Everybody—one way or another—is tempted to give in to de-pression, to quit on life somehow, to weep over helpless situa-tions as I did. I can't go into all the reasons people have for going into their comas of misery. Let me just say that I want to be called The Gloomed One for this commission in order to touch the *gloom side* of all my Care People. The most difficult ones I will have to deal with will be those who are good at heart, and wish every-body else would be the same. So often, the force of their own hopes and ideals push them to have impossible wishes, desiring people and circumstances to be always as perfect as they can be, which, of course, is impossible. Then these vaunted hopes turn to deep, lacklustre depression. Then because of those terrible blind-ers, they cannot do anything except ventilate their anger, outrage, and loneliness.

Some people ritualize this stage—this being possessed by the devil of discouragement—by using drugs and alchohol, or oth-erwise saying no to life; or they become recluses, fixated on only one particular interest or pastime.

Their innate goodness is still there. If only we can reach them with an experience of your love and kindness, Good Father, they will change. I did. And they—once they change—can be so ef-fective healing the soul-sickness of others. That's why A.A. works so well, and all the other mutual-help organizations. It's the old story of "It takes one to know one." A cured melancholic is the best person for helping someone else in its grip.

This is why I want to be called The Gloomed One. My Care People will recognize me as one of them. With the help of Our Lady of Sorrows, and all the saints, we will—little by little—triumph over their defeatism. We'll give them hope again…letting your Son call them by their first names. And in that tender call of Christ, they will find themselves. The eyes of their souls, once released from the blinders of gloom, will discover that their life was right where they had lost it.

Jesus Speaks

It will take some time to get used to your new name, Mary. But I'll try. Father, I ratify The Gloomed One for the appointment of Encourager on the Grand Scale. Let her select as many associates as she needs, who will then canvas the whole world and give hope to the discomfited. My friends here in heaven (who were, at one time, possessed by the devils of discouragement) will heal those similarily afflicted. They will speak to each on a one-to-one basis. If these people, in their pitiable sadness, permit us to do our work, the whole world will experience Easter once again.

God Speaks

So be it. I know this new venture will be a success. I'll make sure of it. After all, to show my compassion and to display my victory over all forms of death is why I sent my son to be Savior in the first place.

Is that not right, my friends?

And all the citizens of heaven respond, "Amen."

9 When Idealism Fades

Ms. Idealzzz

MARY OF BETHANY

When Martha heard that Jesus was coming, she went to meet him. But Mary remained at home. Martha said to Jesus, "Lord, if you had been here, my brother would not have died. But even now, I know that whatever you ask of God, he will give it to you." Jesus said to her, "Your brother will rise." Martha said, "I know that he will rise at the resurrection, on the last day." Jesus said, "I am the resurrection and the life. do you believe this?" She said to him, "Yes, Lord, I believe that you are the Christ, the Son of God...." After Mary had said this, she went away and *quietly called Mary, her sister,* saying, "The Master is here, and calls you...."

John 11:1-44, italics added

Ms. Idealzzz Speaks

My God, I'm not much of a speaker, as you well know, but my sister asked me to speak first for a change, so I will. Martha and I want to team up: she will help extroverts put a little more "inwardness" into their makeup; I'll help the introverts get out of their shell a little more effectively.

We always loved each other—my sister and I—but we did not always understand each other. I was the quiet one, the great idealist. I thought things through and prayed over them until my faith and reason and high principles seemed to fit together. I could devise well-meaning plans for action, but I never did much more than think them through. And I was a good listener, even before I met Jesus, who made me better at it. Anybody with a problem would come to me. Martha was too busy, but I had the time for them. Activity was not my gift. That's why I want to be called "Ms. Idealzzz." The sound of those z's are meant to indicate slumber. I had so many lovely ideals, but I wanted to sleep on them! They were mental edifices of great distinction, but they bore no fruit.

Also, whenever my faith was challenged, I turned into a bowl of gelatin. That happened frequently throughout my life. One of those times was recorded in John's gospel. You know all about it, Father, but I don't think too many others do.

My brother Lazarus was dead and buried. Jesus had not returned from the other side of the Jordan River on time. I couldn't understand why Jesus allowed his good friend to die. He cured others, and he had the time...if he *wanted* to...to come back to Bethany. But he stayed away, deliberately, until Lazarus died!

I was crushed. I didn't want to see anybody, and I had no stomach to help out in any of the arrangements for the wake. (Because my brother was well known and loved and died young, there was a large crowd of mourners.) Martha was stuck with all the burdens of our family responsibilities. I was weeping in my upstairs rooms, oblivious of everyone.

Martha not only did the work, but she was the one with all the faith, too—all the practical faith. As a woman of action, an efficient "doer," she understood Jesus as a man of action. She knew what the Messiah could do if he wanted to. Her own practical virtues nourished her trust in God.

Of course, soon after Lazarus was raised from his death, we both realized why Jesus had delayed coming to our house. He didn't want to simply raise our brother up from his sickbed. If he did, Lazarus would still die...as we all must. Jesus wanted to manifest an infinitely superior gift that he was preparing to give us all: his power over death itself—something more formidable and much more final than a sickbed. By that miracle, Lazarus became the representative of all humanity. His resurrection was the dress rehearsal for Easter's new creation. I realize this, now. But how could I know it before it happened? At the time, I knew only that I felt dead because Lazarus and my hopes were dead. I was in such a morbid state that Martha had to gently pull me out of it. (She did it, as John puts it in the gospel, *quietly*.) I was like someone drunk or drugged; it took a long time for my sister to free me from the self-enclosed prison of crushed hopes.

I think, Good Father, that I can help others who suffer from the same forms of demoralization. The world is so full of idealists like me. They need to know your compassion, so that faith can find a way to get inside their pent-up bitterness. Most of the people I will serve have many good gifts and high ideals. They are often good listeners, very caring people, and (as long as things go right) they manage well.

But when things go wrong—when a member of their family does not live up to their expectations, or when they are treated unjustly in their place of work, or when they are jilted by a friend, or when any number of unexpected frustrations upset their plans—they tend to crumble under the weight of their own heartsickness. Then all those zzz's get tagged on to their ideals, and they end up good for nobody. They close themselves in their darkened bed-rooms (as I did) and want to weep themselves to death.

They need compassion, first. I will remind them of your compassion, Father. They will know the "real you" by the kindness I will offer them...if only they will let me. I will remind them that there is still life and hope. Just because they are rejected, or unjustly treated, or their children won't listen to them, or they miss someone who died—or whatever—this is not the end of the world. Death gives way to the immortality we experience, here, in heaven. The loss of friends can be replaced with others; there are other ways to achieve things, despite tensions at work. You are the source of life, Good Father. Let them remember this, in all their sadness. And let them befriend another person who is more outgoing than they are. As Martha helped me out of my misery, let them go to a friend who is more practical and efficient. They both can work it out together.

Martha will be helping me reach those who are so despondent. She will inspire hope in them. (I will understand them and listen to their problems; my sister will suggest those down-to-earth ways to get out of the hole they are in.) Together, we will be agents of your gentle love—healing the heartsick, coaxing them out of their sulking corners, getting them to "come back downstairs" where Jesus wants to tell them about the new life he has given to Lazarus and to us all.

Jesus Speaks

Of course, I concur. Martha and Mary are two of my best friends. I cannot deny their wishes. They always were good for me: Martha, by her faith and her resolute action; Mary, by her good listening and avid interest in my work. Whenever I could manage, I made it a special point to visit Bethany, just to be with them. Let them be commissioned so that all may enjoy their support, as much as I do.

But please, Father, give me another moment of your eternity to let my apostle Nathaniel have his say.

Nathaniel Speaks

Thank you, my Lord. Good Father, I want to remind the men of earth that Ms. Idealzzz will be an excellent support for them, too. She has a wonderful way of getting men out of their downers. Men don't weep very much when their ideals are blown apart, or when hopes are blasted by injustice. But they do sulk and get sullen; that's as bad as weeping. And when the burden becomes too much, they flare up, sometimes wildly.

They need a good woman to talk to them, like Mary (I mean Ms. Idealzzz); and they need her sister to help them back into the world of production and effective action, a new start.

The sisters of Bethany did it for me so often during those three years. I was an idealist. Jesus first discovered me in the middle of wishful thinking, when I was all alone beside that tree. [John's gospel, chapter 1.] Idealists can get into a lot of depression because of their high hopes. The two Marys—my Lord's Mother and Mary of Bethany—always found a way to get me out of my brooding moods. They listened to me. They changed the focus of my ideals. They can do the same for others. Thank you.

God Speaks

We agree. Let it be done. And Mary, please (now and then) keep me company. I get disheartened, too, at times. I want so much to show the world my love, to treat sinners kindly, to bring life back to those who are sorely distressed. Yet many do not want my help; they block all avenues of compassion. So, in a sense, my hopes and wishes for the world are crushed, at times. I, too, feel jilted. Bring Martha with you, Mary...and every now and then come in to say hello. You are a comfort to me, as well.

Ms. Idealzzz Speaks

My Lord and my God, let it be done to me, according to your will.
The whole company of saints responds, "Amen."

10   When You're Busy as a Bee

THE STORY OF

Ms. Buzzz

MARTHA OF BETHANY

It came to pass, as he continued on his journey to Jerusalem, that Jesus entered a certain village and a woman named Martha welcomed him to her house. She had a sister called Mary, who seated herself at the Lord's feet and listened to his word. But Martha was busy about much serving. And she came up and said, "Lord, is it no concern of yours that my sister has left me to serve alone? Tell her to help me!" But the Lord said, "Martha, Martha, you are anxious and troubled about many things. Few things are needed, *or only one.* Mary has chosen the best part, and it will not be taken away from her."

Luke 10:38-42 ("or only one" is from a Greek manuscript)

Ms. Buzzz Speaks
Good Father, my sister and I always were a team. We want to continue teaming up. Mary concentrates on the introverts. I will work with my kind of people—the doers of good.

Mary's new name is Ms. Idealzzz, with 3 z's in it, to indicate passivity and the lassitude of self-pity. Let me be called, for this commission, "Ms. Buzzz"—a buzzing bee in flight, working feverishly to produce the honey of good.

My Care People are good people, too. They are efficient, able to adjust to new ways of operating, avid for the promotion of all good causes. My People will be managers in business, doctors, supervisors of hospitals, workers for justice (in all its forms), men and women in all roles of leadership. I also include mothers and fathers responsible for bringing up their children and caring for the economics of daily life.

Most of them want to do well. Most of the time, they *do* do well. Then suddenly a problem arises. Employees or fellow workers misunderstand them. Fellow workers show up late for an important meeting; or they get lazy. Children don't help out in their chores. Money problems cause a family crisis. Other unforeseen misfortunes upset the smooth operation of life, which they are used to. Then the negative side of these efficiency experts erupts: they start scolding the lazy or less gifted; they nag their family; they rage against the callousness of the inconsiderate and the wickedness of the unjust.

Luke's gospel mentions one of the times when my mean side became public. Jesus was paying us a visit, the first time in months. I wanted to put on a really nice spread for him. Meals around the campfire can become monotonous after a while. I was sure he'd like my home cooking—everything from scratch.

As it turned out (I learned the hard way) he did *not* want a big meal. He was going to Jerusalem to suffer and die. His heart was heavy and his thoughts about his "hour," soon to come, had taken away his appetite. He wanted to talk, but not even the apostles would listen to him. They wanted a militant Messiah, one who would establish a mighty kingdom of peace by means of conquests and clever politics. It was not to be that way.

Only with us could he talk about his high purposes. He hoped to relax with us...to lay down his burdens for a while...to find some sympathy and understanding.

My sister was willing to do this. She was always a good listener. I couldn't—I didn't want to, either. But even if I did, I couldn't. My flag of action was up; plans were made. My recipies were prepared, and no matter what, we *were* going to have that big supper! Mary tried to persuade me to wait until Jesus arrived, to be sure about what he wanted. I was too busy to think about any plans but my own. When Jesus said he just wanted to talk, I dismissed his words as mere politeness, and then excused myself to the kitchen. I expected my sister to follow me. She didn't, but stayed right there in the living room, listening to Jesus' words.

I was getting madder by the minute. I started knocking pans around—noisily!—so that Mary would get the point. That didn't work. After an hour of doing everything myself, I really got angry. I stormed back into the room and scolded Mary for being so lazy and thoughtless. I did so indirectly...asking Jesus to give the reprimand. Being a good administrator in every sense of the word, I thought that every person ought to be just like me, giving highest priority to efficient operation.

The Lord put me in my place. I was crushed. But I was the hostess, after all. When Jesus said what he did—in the way he did—I put the food on hold, took off my apron, and sat beside my sister. Sometimes, prayer and good listening are higher on the scale of priorities.

Little by little, I entered into their mood of prayer. As we listened to the unfolding of events (Jesus was telling us what had already taken place and what would soon be coming up) we understood the seriousness of it all. We gave Jesus our compassion. We entered into the mood of the moment, appreciating his nobility of purpose and high resolve of love.

I think we were really the first ones (after his own mother) to understand just who Jesus really was, and why he must do what he did. Our acceptance and our sisterly love kept him going.

I learned, then, that there are different ways to "get going." With my extrovert focus and my emphasis on action, I always thought "get going" meant "prepare the meal, win the game,

solve the problem, make the business run better, succeed...succeed
...succeed!"

Sometimes it's not any of these things. "Get going" can also
mean keeping hopes alive, praying about something, taking more
time to think about whether all this pushing yourself and others is
worth it...things like that. Sometimes, the right thing to do is *not*
to do. It is to delay activity and listen more...and maybe put more
balance into a workaholic's world.

That's what it is all about: balance. That's why my sister and I
want to team up. I will help Mary with the introverts, who sometimes get into a mood of weeping and moping around, letting
their ideals crash over their heads. I'll help to give these people a
push, a new plan of action, hopefulness, perhaps more energetic
resolve. Mary will help me with my extroverts, those who sometimes get on everybody's backs (and on their own) when activity
is frustrated and work bogs down...and especially when work is
not called for.

Together we will remind the "pressure people" of the work
world to calm down, to play more, to cultivate the inward activities that open up the world of beauty, art, prayer, and having en-
joyment.

Father, we want them to slow down enough so that they may
feel your kindness and compassion. Once they understand that
your love can override all frustrations, they will see things on a
larger scale, and be more pliant, less pushy. They will be more
patient with the inefficient people who have a slower tempo. In a
word, they'll scold less, love more.

Jesus Speaks
Of course, I ratify. Ms. Idealzzz and Ms. Buzzz will do good
work. They did for me. They were two of my dearest friends.

And Father, if I may, I want to recall the lovely evening I spent
after my resurrection. This is not mentioned in the gospels. It was
a private affair. My Mother was with me; we joined Martha,
Mary, and Lazarus. Our supper that night was a "rain check" in a
way. It made up for the meal I did not want to eat when I was on
my way to Jerusalem some months before.

The evening I speak of was a most memorable time. Martha was at her best, a charming hostess. Mary was a delight; she brought out lively conversation in us all. In the hours that followed supper, we collaborated on a plan, a kind of rough draft of the schedule that all my disciples would take part in, once the church got going. It had a fine balance between times for work and prayer, for the worship of God and recreation, for preaching to the people and the teaching of the young. It became the original blueprint for the first community of believers. Martha and Mary did most of the planning. My Mother, Lazarus, and I just added our suggestions now and then.

Martha and Mary can do this for everybody. Balance is their combined talent, most of all. Balance they can give to both the over-organized and the underachievers. I'm so glad they volunteered.

God Speaks

It pleases me, as well. One special favor I ask of you, Martha. I want you to work with the workaholics of the world and get me out of the rut so many have put me in. I speak of some parents, teachers, preachers, clergy, and others who hold positions of authority...and are personally dedicated to high achievement. That's fine, in itself. But when this virtue mixes with pride and pressure-to-function-perfectly, it influences them to make me into a scold, a nag, a "deity of displeasure" who is unhappy about the way imperfect humans are messing up the works.

Of course, I am the judge, and will be at the end of time. And such things as sins and condemnation of unrepentant sinners exist. And I do get very angry when people refuse to forgive others, after I sent my Son to forgive them. Also, it saddens me grievously when iniquity abounds.

But that is not all I am. I am compassion, too, and patient kindness. I don't want people to think of me as that horrible Santa Claus song puts it, "He's making a list/and checking it twice/to see whether you've/been naughty or nice!"

No! It's the efficient people in the world, with their propensity to put projects over people, who try to use me as their "scolding machine"...as they try to force others to shape up to their standards. I don't want to be feared as some monster who is forever "making a list" of faults so that I can punish people. I want to be loved as their Good Father. If you influence those people who want everybody to function perfectly—to come down from their high demands and develop more patience and kindness—I will begin to be better understood.Thanks for this, Ms. Buzzz. Thanks, ahead of time. We'll be in touch.

Both Martha and Mary say, "So be it, Lord."

All the citizens of heaven say, "Amen."

11 Being a Good Listener

Mrs. Flexible

SAINT ELIZABETH

[The angel said to Mary:] "Elizabeth, your cousin, also has conceived a son in her old age...." [So] Mary went with haste into the hill country to a town of Juda. And she entered the house of Zechariah and saluted Elizabeth. When Elizabeth heard Mary's greeting, the babe in her womb danced for joy. And Elizabeth was filled with the Holy Spirit and cried out in a loud voice, saying, "Blessed are you among women; and blessed is the fruit of your womb! And how have I deserved that the mother of my Lord should come to me."   Luke 1:36, 39-47

Mrs. Flexible Speaks
God, my Father, I want to follow the sisters of Bethany. My role, for all my Care People, will be to add another dimension to the link between compassion and good listening. I ask for the duration of this commission to be called "Mrs. Flexible."

In the gospel of St. Luke, I am placed in a heroic role. Instead of talking about myself and my baby, I step down and praise Mary and honor her child. St. Luke does not mention how difficult it was for me to act this way; only you know the struggle I had, patient Father. Let me tell the court about it.

I guess I always was a good person and praised for my diligence. Since childhood, I fitted in. I became a good wife; and as years followed years, I learned the pattern of what was expected of me. Then I made that pattern my own. I don't think I was ever actually a dictator of the house, but I was bossy: I talked a lot...and I expected people to agree with my ideas and to carry out my suggestions. From the moment I hit upon a practical plan for doing something, or thought about something worth mentioning, it was very difficult for anyone or anything to change my mind.

You may now understand, from what I have said, that it was not an easy time for me, once I became pregnant with John. Oh, I marveled at the miracle that in my advanced age the Lord God graced me with a child. I never ceased to be grateful for the gift of life. But it was frustrating to feel so lonely. I had no one to talk to, no one to help me through the pregnancy.

My neighbors were nice enough...in the beginning. They wished me well and praised God that my prayers were answered. But they had their own concerns. (And I suspect they were a little jealous that my husband and I had been singled out so specially. They always seemed to have some reason for excusing themselves quite promptly from my company.)

My husband was no help. After the angel made him mute, it seemed his ears went, too. He would just go for long walks, and once inside he would brood a lot. He did what I asked him to do and we got along, but he was no company really.

So it should surprise no one that I was overjoyed when I learned that my cousin Mary was coming to see me. I started planning the details of our visit right away: how I would tell her all that had happened in the last few months, how I was preparing for my child's birth, what things I needed in the way of baby clothes. There were so many things I wanted to say to her and brag about, so many worries to share with her. Mary was the kind of woman who would really hear me out.

She finally arrived. I remember taking a deep breath as I prepared to gush out everything I had been storing up, just as soon as she took off her cloak. Then something happened. At the very instant of our greeting my baby began stirring in my womb. I felt as though he were dancing. Ordinarily all this movement would have caused me pain or frightened me. But it didn't. I felt that if my baby could be given a voice he would shout Alleluia! The sense of his joy flooded me with joy. But it was more than that; it was grandeur, high mystery. I felt that all the majestic movements experienced by Abraham, Moses, David, Judith, Esther, and all the saints of old were compressed in the my baby' dance.

Then for the first time in my life I bent my own purposes. I became flexible. I scuttled all the things I was going to do, all the speeches I had saved up. I simply hugged my cousin and looked at her with love. I became oblivious of myself, filled only with reverence for her. She had an aura about her. I had often been filled with awe during moments of quiet prayer when I accompanied Zechariah to the temple and paid tribute to Yahweh in the women's court. But this encounter with the mystery of God's love, this meeting with my Lord, was greater and deeper than anything experienced before.

Years later my son pointed to Jesus and said, "He must increase; I must decrease." I felt the same. Instinctively I decided to change my plans to blurt out everything about me and my child. Mary and her child must increase.

I praised Mary to high heaven and took her hands in mind. I showed her that I understood all her deep secrets. Then she was free enough with me to be able to sing her song about God's love.

And you all know what happened after that. Being more flexible, I began to notice gestures and thought about what they meant. I observed whether a person's eyes sparkled with interest or were lidded with the look of boredom. I paid more attention to my own body and to the surroundings—indeed, to all the providential ways that you, Father, might be telling me to adapt my plans. I enjoyed life more once I became less unbending in the demands I put on others and myself. I could be more compassionate toward everyone. And so, of course, I could better appreciate kindness wherever it came from.

Good Father, my own story of Mary's visitation sums up the special area of my concern. My Care People will be those who cannot easily adapt to unforeseen circumstances. These are good people for the most part; they mean well and help others in many ways. But they can be pushy and talk a lot, and they sometimes fail to notice mood shifts and the meaning that may be implied in every chance interruption.

I will be their friend. I won't lecture them. (Lecturers never like to be lectured to.) With your grace, Father, I will help them feel what I felt when John danced in my womb. With my help, they will become more sensitive to change, more sympathetic to the unspoken needs of others, more patient with their fast-paced priorities and preoccupations.

Once they become flexible, they will be able to balance talking with listening, planning with adjusting, working with waiting. Then all the good aspects of their personality will improve, and they will discover great joy in supportive friendships such as they never had before.

It has happened to me. I have thrilled with the joy that accompanies God's love ever since the visitation of my cousin. And now I have this abundant joy in heaven. If I may, I want to help others experience the same.

Jesus Speaks

Father, I've been watching my mother ever since Aunt Elizabeth began. Please let her speak for both of us.

Mary Speaks

Of course. My Son and I champion the cause of my cousin's new mission. The need is there. Good people have to temper the good they do with compassion for the people they intend to help. And those individuals graced with the ability to talk well, who are full of plans and purpose and interesting agenda, have to develop more sensitivity for the people they are talking to. They cannot look on their friends as an unregarded blur, as though they existed only to function as an audience.

My visit with Elizabeth was one of the happiest times in my life, thanks to her sensitivity and compassion. As you know, Father, there was no doubt about my trust in you. Ever since the angel Gabriel told me your plan of love, I was willing to do whatever you wanted. The doubts I had were about myself. I wondered whether I could do all that was expected of me as mother of the Messiah. I wondered what kind of a Messiah he would be. How would his role as Savior take shape? Would he be another Abraham? Someone like Moses? A king like David? A suffering servant like Jeremiah? How would his own people receive him? And how dare I discipline a child who is the Son of God? Should I treat him with love and firmness, rules and flexibility, like a normal boy? What?

These quandaries were buzzing around my head, as I headed south to see my cousin. She was such a good friend to me, such a good listener and support. I was the same for her. It was in the little things we did together that we learned to have more confidence in the role we were to play as part of the great mystery of your love.

Cooking meals and making clothes, praying the psalms, and talking together on the porch as the sun went down—all this was a delight. For me, Elizabeth was like a harvester who stores enough grain for a long winter. She filled my heart with joy. Thanks to her confidence in me, I had confidence in the future. Good memories of her compassion kept me going during my bouts with sorrow. She will do the same for all who ask her to. Let her begin her marvelous style of supportive friendship.

God Speaks

So be it. My dear Elizabeth, proceed. Just one more point. Remember to be flexible toward the other extreme of personality too. Some individuals are too sensitive about what happens when change comes up. With these, a frown or some other gesture indicating boredom crushes them. They become afraid to speak up lest they cause displeasure. These people need to be more resourceful and courageous. Ask your son to help you with this group, Elizabeth. John the Baptist was as forthright as they come. If the truth were at stake, he didn't care how many toes he stepped on. Here, as is the case so often, balance is what is needed. Soften the strong so that they may bend better. Then strengthen the sensitive so that they may be more resolute.

You'll do fine, you and John. You always have. I love you. My love will stay you firm and stretch you flexible.

All the citizens of heaven respond, "Amen."

12 Dealing With Violence

Rachael

A SISTER OF ONE OF THE BOYS BUTCHERED

Herod, seeing that he had been tricked by the Magi, was exceedingly angry. And he slew all the boys of Bethlehem and its neighborhood who were two years old or under....Then was fulfilled what was spoken through Jeremiah the prophet: "A voice was heard in Rama, weeping and loud lamentations: it is Rachael, weeping for her children. She is inconsolable because they are no more." Matthew 2:16-18

Rachael Speaks
Father, I'm not at all sure I will do any good, make any impression. The people I want to touch with your compassion are the hardest to reach. I speak in behalf of all battered people in the world: battered children, wives bruised by their husbands (and vice versa), those who witnessed tragedy, survivors of concentration camps or vile prisons, hostages, the tortured, indeed all who endured brutality of any kind.

For this commission, Father, I want to be called "Rachael," which is my real name, as you know. It is also my signature, in a representative way. Everyone will know what I mean once they understand that St. Matthew used Abraham's wife Rachael to summarize all the woe that resulted from the exile of the Chosen People to Babylon. Rachael wept because all her children were driven from the land. My own family wept when we watched those fourteen baby boys (my little brother was one of them) beheaded by Herod's soldiers.

I was seven years old at the time. Rough hands forced my eyes to watch the horrible scene. I shrieked. I could not comprehend such vicious behavior. Then I sobbed uncontrollably and neither ate nor spoke for days. Only by your grace, Father, did I continue to live. I know I did not want to. I was in a daze for a year or more, but eventually my tears dried up. Even so, I still cannot forget that massacre. My life was scarred. All through my teens and early twenties I was afraid of every harsh noise, every utterance of anger, every hint of a fight or war. Fortunately, I married a gentle husband.

I hated you, God my Father, for the longest time. You know this, yet you were so patient with me. I could not understand how a good God would permit such ruthless butchery. My brother was only thirteen months old. You created him for life, then you let his head be severed before he even learned to speak.

I forgot exactly when my anger against you began to be healed. It wasn't until my mid-30s that I started thinking about what my bitterness was doing to me. The turning point came during one of your Son's last sermons. Near the end of his ministry he was talking about forgiveness, how we must look into the warped nature of our own vindictiveness before we judge the actions of another. I had hated Jesus, too, passionately...up until that afternoon. I had blamed him for the death of my baby brother. After all, I said, if it weren't for Herod's jealousy of Jesus, my brother would not have been killed!

What the Lord said that day in Jerusalem hit me hard. I realized that in my own way I was as bad as Herod. I was nursing my own grudges against other people. Just a few months before, I had lashed out against an ex-friend of mine who did me an injustice. I was a "small-time Herod." When I finally realized this, I became disgusted with myself.

These new insights made me think of you in a different light, good Father. You no more caused the death of my brother than you caused my ex-friend to suffer from my spitefulness. It was people, with their hateful nature, who did the dirty work—both times. But I still didn't have an answer to the problem of death. The only thing I had was the conviction that God will not intrude on our free will. If Herod or I decided to use our free will in the pursuit of ruthlessness, God won't interfere. Well, this let God off the hook (pardon me for speaking so freely, Father), but it did not change anything. It only redirected blame.

Then two years later the apostle John came to Bethlehem, preaching the resurrection of our Lord. He told us what Jesus' life, death, life-again meant to all of us. This put a new dimension on all my thoughts about death. My brooding now had a different backdrop. John told us what the Lord said about his leaving and preparing a place for us. John told us most convincingly how certain he was that the fourteen boys of Bethlehem, killed some 30 years earlier, were enjoying perfect happiness in the place Jesus prepared for them.

Everything then fell into place. I was wrestling with the word "why" for so long. Why did my brother have to die? Why must I die? Why does a loving God let death be the doom of everything? When John and I talked in private, he shifted my question from "why?" to "how?" And then to "what then?" He told me how Jesus died for us and rose from death to a fuller life, richer with beauty, better than it was before. And he promised to be with us forever and bring us into a new lifestyle, with all our curses gone, and all our questions answered, where brutality will never take place again.

The "what then?" is where I am now, with all of you, and with my baby brother, too. For the life of me, I cannot understand why so many humans scoff at our existence, calling it "pie in the sky." Christ's gift of paradise is not just a pious sentiment said to mourners because no one knows what else to say. It is the truth. And it is the only way anyone can make sense of the fact of death or the tragic consequences of violence. You, Father, are the God of life and love. Could you possibly contradict yourself by giving life and then taking it away? By giving love and then letting the object of your love moulder in a grave, to be forgotten? Sometimes the most important thing in life is to ask the right questions. And now, thank heaven, it is very good to live here, with all the right answers. As you know, Father, I was able to help many people in Judea wrestle with the problem of death. And I comforted, sometimes even healed, my neighbors in Bethlehem who were still bitter about Herod's atrocity.

I want to do all that I can to help the people who are suffering today. I'll work with other saints to comfort those who are so wounded by battered-child experiences that they (like me for so long) might just as well be dead. We want everyone who is so afflicted to experience your compassion, Father. Heaven's dimension of eternity should lighten the burden of human fears.

My Care People will be the vicitms of atrocities and those who witnessed the atrocities. More often than not, some experiences are worse than death itself: child beatings, youth pornography, incest, and other cruelties that scar the memory for life and stifle the ability to lead productive lives.

I won't be able to reach them all. I know this. Some are so bitter and cynical that love has no place in their lives. But I will help some of them. I will tell them of Jesus' lessons about forgiveness and free will. I will open up the prospect of life after death in heaven, where wounds will all be healed.

Please, Father, grace me with this appointment. There are so many heart-bruised people on earth, I want to start as soon as I can.

Jesus Speaks
By all means, Father, let her begin. In the meantime, I will do what I can to influence friends of the battered people, so that all who have been hurt like Rachael will find support in the compassion of friends and family. Only when they experience human compassion can they then learn to understand ours. Only when they experience both sources of compassion will they finally discover hope and gentle love.

God Speaks
So be it. You will have a full workload, Rachael. And do not become discouraged. Bitterness of soul is the most formidable obstacle of all.

I know you will be busy, but I want to add one other group of women for your concern. This is in the general area of battered children. I want you to help the culprits in this case, not the victims. The victims of abortion are now with us. These unborn babies are as innocent as were the fourteen boys of Bethlehem. I gave them life. I mean them to live. I won't turn them away just because humans did not want them. They are all fine.

It is their mothers, and sometimes their fathers, who concern me. When they allowed their babies to be aborted, in many, many instances they weren't in their right minds. They were pressured, scared, distraught, hurting greatly.

Then comes afterwards, sometimes years later, they feel very guilty; their guilt is heavier than any guilt I could put on them, even if I wanted to. Please, Rachael, go to them. Tell them of my compassion. I forgive them. They must get on with the job of living. They have responsibilities—other children, other people in their lives. Let them remember me as the God of life and love, and do your best to get them out of the deathtraps of their past. The only healthy way to remember their sins is to be compassionate with the sins of others, as I have been compassionate with them. They should be patient with others, remembering that they are sinners, too.

Their life on earth is too short to dwell on death or self-inflicted shame. And our life here is too long to let anything but love be present.

Do what you can, Rachael. Soothe them with your kindly ways. I will be with you.

And the saints respond, "So shall we all. Amen."

13 When Regrets Come to Haunt You

THE STORY OF

Grets

MOTHER OF THE MAN BORN BLIND

The Pharisees did not believe that the man had been blind and had got his sight back.... [So] they called the parents of the man and questioned them saying, "Is this your son? Was he born blind? How, then, does he now see?" His parents answered them and said, "We know this is our son and that he was born blind. But how he now sees we do not know, or who opened his eyes we do not know. Ask him. He is of age. Let him speak for himself." ...These things his parents said because they feared the leaders of the Jews. For it was already decided that if anyone were to confess Jesus to be the Christ, he should be put out of the Synagogue. This is why his parents said, "He is of age. Ask him."   John 9:1-40

Grets Speaks
Father, call me "Grets." I used to be filled with *re*grets about my life, but that is all behind me. I no longer rehash old mistakes and sins. I'm living in the present, and it feels great.

I've wanted to speak up ever since the mother of the bride at Cana began these interviews. It seems that both of us were oversensitive to what other people think. Indeed, like so many people, we were addicted to peer pressure.

Mrs. What of Cana was worried about her future: What would

the neighbors say when they learn that the wedding reception had to end early because of a lack of wine? My troubles were different. They came later on, after I caved in to the negative pull of society.

You already know the whole story, Father: the anxieties that badgered me, my deplorable behavior. But most of the saints here don't know about it. I am still embarrassed by my weakness. But now I realize that the honest admission of my mistakes can help others, so I want to tell it the way it happened.

Reuben was my only son, a blessing to my husband and me. He was also a worry and a burden. Because he was born blind, we cared for him for 38 years, and even set him up in the begging business. All those years we prayed for a healing. And then it came. We were overjoyed when he rushed home to show us. He looked at us with the brightest, most beautiful dark eyes, as he told us how Jesus freed him from his blindness. He could walk by himself in traffic, get a real job, look upon our faces, and see all the beautiful things he had missed. It was wonderful at first.

We hurried to get the necessary things ready to offer our sacrifice of praise in the temple. Before we left home, however, neighbors came with ominous news that carried a vicious threat some Pharisees made: If we publicly praised God and celebrated Jesus' miracle, we would be ostracized from society. If we didn't knuckle under to those who held real power, we could be barred from the synagogue. Now that might not mean much to people today, who might think that being refused permission to enter church or synagogue is no big thing. After all, they would have more time for themselves on Sunday or the Sabbath. But ours was a closed society, much like the Amish people of today. We, like them, feared the "shunning" more than we did death itself. It could mean loneliness and impoverishment. Not to worship also meant not shopping, not buying or selling property, not socializing with anyone. Our neighbors would ignore us; our credit would be no good. Every possible obstacle would be put in our path. By decree of some powerful Pharisees, we would become nobodies, with no rights.

We couldn't stand up to that. We surrendered our joy, our

right to celebrate, our desire to thank God for the miracle of our son's eyesight. Instead, we went along with what they wanted; we didn't want to get involved. My husband and I were like prisoners of war, giving our captors nothing but our name, rank, and serial number. We acknowledged that he was our son, that he was born blind, and that he is blind no longer. Then we begged them not to ask us any more questions—we did not want to make waves.

Well, that surrender to the pressure of the powerful kept us "safe." We remained accepted members of society, for a while. Life went on as before. We could still shop freely and take part in our normal routine. But our son was disgusted with us. He left home to follow Jesus. Can't say that we blamed him. We gave him our blessing. My husband and I were already feeling the pressure of trying to live, without harm, in both worlds. We knew we were appeasers, and we didn't like ourselves.

Meanwhile, our son joined the disciples, as I said. He was the errand boy at first, later developing into a very good preacher. He also concentrated on helping the blind recuperate after the Lord healed them. Like most of the disciples (as distinct from those who were called apostles), his work was on a part-time basis. Sometimes he was with us at home.

We were so glad he did not forsake us, although we had grown more and more disgusted with ourselves. We felt like traitors in both camps. As the rift between the Lord and the Pharisees grew wider and more menacing, we acted out our allegiance to Jesus' enemies, but our heart was with the Messiah and his beautiful truth. Our heart was, but our pocketbook was still on the side of the powerful. And we wanted so much to "belong," not to be different.

We couldn't stand our fence-straddling any longer. The break came on Good Friday morning. We had joined the ranks of all those who were told to swell the chorus of "Crucify Jesus the Nazarene!" The Chief Priest and the Pharisees ordered us all to be in the courtyard—or else. We looked at Jesus, standing forlorn next to Pilate, beaten and jeered at. Then we remembered what he had done for our son, and we felt sick to our stomachs. We went home, packed up, and left for Damascus where we had relatives.

We followed our hearts at last. When we heard Paul preach some years later, we finally had the courage of our convictions.

The rest is part of our happy ending, as you know, Father. We no longer felt compelled to place such high importance on the world's approval. We received the fruits of your acceptance.

We want to be "change agents" for the Care People we will focus on. Of course, some of the people my husband and I have in mind cannot change what has happened to them in their past. Some have AIDS, and that does not have an antidote; not yet anyway. Some are afflicted with drug addiction, alcoholism, or some other compulsion. Any of these addictions can incapacitate a person much more forcibly than the addiction for security that afflicted us. But we will do what we can to help them change their attitude about their sad situations.

Another large area of Care People will be among the teenagers and pre-teens. Many of their groups force standards of behavior on their members with the threat of exclusion that is even more formidable than the pressure we succumbed to. If they don't go along, they can be more than objects of contempt, they can be fugitives of fear.

In the work world, too, there are many kinds of behavior manipulation: employees must adhere to their superiors' illicit demands for sexual favors or double-dealing—or else! Sometimes the same thing applies among fellow workers: some union leadership has a tradition of underhanded deals, and they will not allow any whistle-blower to cross them. These are some of the people that my husband and I will try to reach. We will do what we can to bring them all the hope of heaven.

People become addicted because of caving in to the pressure of other "authorities." We want to help them, too. Sometimes the "authority" is their friends, or peers, or even the repetitive advertising over the media. Sexual promiscuity, drinks, or drugs can become the "in thing." People can start stealing or killing just to get the "right kind" of clothes. If they don't conform to what their peers demand, they are excluded from their society. So they succumb and are hooked on whatever it is. They are miserable and their life is filled with regrets.

All these people cannot understand the word "compassion"; they have seen so little of it in their lifetimes. Simplistic slogans like "Just say no" and "Drugs are garbage" fill them with more bitterness. Their plight is a complex affliction—physical dependence, emotional slavery, spiritual guilt—and they are treated with patronizing disdain. They need a deep-down healing, Father, to turn their life around; they need to experience compassion in its dearest form. I want them all to feel what my husband and I felt on that Good Friday when Jesus, Son of God, sent by your love, died on a cross for all. He did not knuckle under to the world's opinion. He did not drink the wine to dull his pain. He suffered. With his last breath, he urged you, Father, to pardon our sins, to free us from the destructive addictions in our lives.

Please, my God, let me minister to these people. I'll find a way to show them the compassion of your son and be a mainstay for their encouragement. I know there will be many failures; addicts and others driven by guilt who are not always agreeable to grace. I will get discouraged by my own track record at times. Those who cheer up others need to be cheered up themselves; those who encourage others need to be encouraged, too. So I ask you to appoint a support group for me, saints who will counsel me and help me to be patient, and teach me how to live with sometimes failing. Thank you.

Jesus Speaks
Yes, by all means, let her begin. I love Grets. (I like your name, too, by the way.) I noticed her Good Friday morning. Up there on the palace steps with Pilate, I had a pretty good view of everybody in the crowd, I saw where she was, near the back, with her husband. Their faces were as pale as porcelain and their shoulders were hunched up with anger at the malice of the crowd. They left defiantly, shaking their fists at the Pharisees who were writing down their names.

I want her husband to help her. And I appoint my apostle Philip to select a group of friends for her. Philip is an encourager too. He will be a wise counsellor, Grets. He knows the pitfalls of discouragement. (He has tripped over almost all of them!) He will be compassionate toward you in the arduous mission you volunteered for; he will see to it that you do not lose heart. And I shall be with you. The love and the life I gave when I was crucified has not diminished. Not one bit. In heaven we are outside earth-bound time, but we are not aloof from it. My Good Friday compassion is alive to every moment of every person's torment. This love of mine will live more strongly in your heart, too, because of your new work on this commission. Begin.

God Speaks
Yes, Grets, begin with our blessing and encouragement. One suggestion: Form a sub-committee of saints, a large one that will concentrate on another group of people suffering from regrets.

Your concern will be those who succumbed to peer pressure and addictive behavior, which is a field vast enough to tax all of your patience. There are others burdened with a different kind of emotional drain. I will call their affliction "nostalgic enervation." Many people look back on their past and wish they had lived it differently. It's that big "if" that drains their energy. *If* I only took that job when it was offered. *If* I only married her, or him. *If* I only didn't let so-and-so talk me out of my decision to go someplace else, or to stay where I was.

On and on the litany of lapsed chances goes. Everybody thinks of these fantasies at times; that's human. But some get so obsessed by their missed opportunities there's hardly any energy left for living in the real world, with their actual family, friends, and fellow workers.

Do what you can, Grets. My saints will help you. I don't want anyone to miss life and love because they are swallowed up by past regrets. I don't want them to miss heaven for anything in the world.

Let us all say "Amen" to this, together. (And so they do.)

14 When You Pray and Pray, But Nothing Happens

Patience

THE LONG-AFFLICTED WOMAN

There was a woman who for 18 years had had a sickness. She was bent over and utterly unable to look upwards. When Jesus saw her he laid his hands upon her and instantly she was made straight. The Lord answered [those who were indignant that he cured the woman on the Sabbath]: Hypocrites! Does not each of you loose his ox or ass from the manger and lead it forth for water on the Sabbath? And this woman, daughter of Abraham as she is, whom Satan has bound for 18 years, ought not she be loosed from her bond on the Sabbath? Luke 13:10-17

Patience Speaks
Good Father, as you know, I was never very good with words. I would not dare to explain, as though mere words could do it, the greatest mystery in the world: why a good God permits the innocent to suffer, to languish in a sickbed, to be permanently crippled, unable to control the ordinary events of their lives. Why does a good God allow individuals to be born with brain damage? Why do freak accidents or crippling diseases snuff out all chance for a normal life? Why does God seem to turn a deaf ear to all the heart-felt prayers for a miracle? Why do certain people

suffer so much, while others who have no faith and little love grow up strong and healthy and get all the breaks? This is the great mystery that I will never try to explain. People who suffer from these evils need compassion, not explanations. Besides, Good Father, you never did solve the problem of evil and suffering. You inspired prophets to grapple with the mystery, but they never gave a really satisfactory answer. You then sent your only Son, not only to undo evil, but to overcome it. He lived in a world of gross injustice and suffered the full brunt of evil. He was wickedly condemned, brutally mistreated, and died young.

Being nailed to the cross was a disability far worse than my 18 years of existing in a hunchback position. Jesus' crucifixion was so great an evil that the sun went in hiding and tombs of rock refused to hold their dead. He was the ultimate victim of every evil, ever. But Jesus did not stay a corpse. He was raised from the dead, as he promised. He told everyone he would link his risen body to us all, and prepare a place for us in heaven where evil would harm us no longer.

This must become the practical consideration for all who suffer from the hopelessness of their painful situations. If earth were all there was, the pitiful endurance of the disabled would not make sense. Only the backdrop of eternity can mold a dreary future into one of hope.

Meanwhile people must continue to suffer, to endure, to wish for better. That was all I could do those 18 long years. I was often dejected because of my condition. Then after Jesus cured me, I remained bitter and cynical. I complained of what my parents and I called the "too patient patience" of God's providence. That is a long time to waste away. Eighteen years.

Jesus knew about me right from the beginning. You know all about it, Father. I brought it to your attention often enough. But let me tell the entire court. Mary and I were playmates. When we were young I would stay at her house so that my parents could go to Jerusalem. The next year Mary would stay at my house. And we did a lot together. We were, still are, dear, dear friends. I was 29 years old when the sickness crippled my backbone. I cried often and wanted to die. It was painful to walk and I could see nothing but my feet—nobody's face, never their eyes. The only way I could look at the world was lying down, sidewards. I needed great care. Eating was a long and tedious task. I prayed, we all prayed, that God would cure me. They carried me to the famous healing pool in the Holy City. Nothing happened. Nothing ever happened.

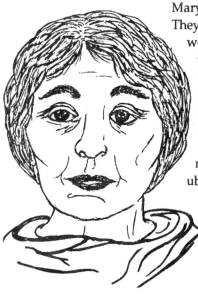

Mary and Joseph visited me often. They prayed, too, but their prayers weren't answered either. Then after 18 years, Jesus effortlessly changed my life around. At last, I could walk and dance and see the world straight in the eye.

For the first few days of my new-found health, I was exuberantly happy. Jesus took my side against the Pharisees. He dignified me, calling me daughter of Abraham. He honored me higher than all God's creatures. And he said (I'll never forget the tenderness in his eyes) I ought to be rescued from my affliction, after all that time.

A few weeks later I became morose. I asked myself, "Since Jesus easily healed me that Sabbath day, why didn't he do it sooner? Since he had kept such good track of all my years of frustration, why didn't he shorten that time and quietly cure me ten years earlier? Or even before that?"

Mary told me some of the reasons why. Her son could not begin his miracles until the Father gave him the go-ahead. The cures he lavished on the people during his three-year ministry were signs pointing to something more. In my case, he didn't straighten up my back earlier because even though he was a friend of my family, he was the Messiah first. His power to heal me was a message about salvation; it was not an orthopedic short-cut.

I understood at last. My story, in all its unique particulars, won't help those who are still suffering. The facts of my hardships and healing belong to me alone. I cannot change the severity of anybody else's pain, but I can change their feelings about those hurts. That is why I want to be called "Patience" for this commission. My Care People will be all those who see themselves fitting into my story in some way.

Patients are who they are. Patience is what they need. I can feel with them in their affliction, their frustrations and fears. I know well their loneliness because they are different from others, and the borderline despair that taunts their hopelessness.

I will not preach to them. I wouldn't dare tell them to cheer up. I just want to suggest other feelings for their downcast hearts. If they can become aware of your compassion, Father, your special love for them (like Jesus' special love for me), they will see some good come out of their worst adversity.

They can do much good for others because of their afflictions. (People listen better to appeals for patience coming from those who are suffering themselves.) They can heal divisiveness in their families and be a source of courage for all who suffer in any way.

I want to be with them, Father. I cannot hold their hands, but I can touch their hearts. My feelings will be one with theirs. They will learn compassion from the way they suffer. And they will have enough hope to get them home—with us in heaven.

Jesus Speaks
Yes, Father, let Patience be so assigned. I know first-hand how she suffered those 18 years. We talked many times for long hours. She knows what it is to undergo protracted pain and fear and the dreariness of the same old thing day after day. She will help many by the good nursing of her compassion and prepare them well for death. Then after death she will guide them here where fear will be no more, and the 18 years of hardship will seem as nothing compared to the healthy goodness of our whole forever.

God Speaks
So be it. One further item. I want to give full coverage for all who

are involved in suffering: the families who care for the disabled, doctors and nurses, nurses aides, social workers, volunteers—all who visit, all who are in any way a part of the anguish of the afflicted. They need patience too. The mood of despair brought on by protracted affliction and the sense of helplessness can get the best of people down. Your parents helped you all those years, Patience. Mary did too. They will continue to give the nurturers all that they need to keep them going and not lose heart. The givers of constant care must be cheerful givers. Therefore, let this courtesy begin with us. What say you all?

And the angels and saints of heaven reply, "Amen."

15 Feeling Like a Nobody

THE STORY OF

Justa

SUSANNA, ONE OF THE PROVIDERS

With Jesus were the twelve apostles and certain women who had been cured of evil spirits and infirmities. Mary who is called the Magdalene, from whom seven devils had gone out; and Joanna, the wife of Chusa, Herod's steward; and Susanna; and many others who used to provide for them out of their means.   Luke 8:1-3

Justa Speaks

This won't take long, Good Father. I want to be one of the people volunteering for your compassionate committee. I always was an "also ran" kind of person. I want to give grace and endurance to the "also rans" who are still in the majority on earth.

Please call me "Justa," without a last name, without a prefix; just "Justa." That's how I always thought of myself. In school I was "just another schoolgirl." Then I got married and Joshua and I had children. I understood my role. When people asked me who I was, I would instinctively reply that I was "just a housewife." Some would call me a drudge. I wasn't, really. A drudge implies that I was resentful. That was not so, not for the most part. I fitted into things. On the flat side of my personality, life was rather boring. Predictable. I often envied lives that were more exciting. On the good side, I was a calming influence for my husband and those three children of mine, all of whom had short tempers. I helped them collect their ruffled emotions and control their sometimes unmanageable tempers.

I think I did a reasonably good job. Nothing noteworthy. Ordinary days followed, one after another, without too many surprises. My husband died rather early, but we managed. The children married young. My role of "just a housewife" became "just me." I anticipated joining the ranks of "just a grandmother, babysitter for my family," but something inside said I should not end my days like that. Oh, I loved my grandchildren, and they loved me. But enough is enough. I grew tired of being an afterthought to everybody else's life.

Jesus' mother and I have been friends since childhood, ever since our school days in Jerusalem. She asked me to join a band of women who were forming a kind of auxiliary group for Jesus and the apostles. Mary herself would stay at home. because she didn't want to influence her son too much. She knew that Jesus must continue his work according to the unmixed directives of his Father's Spirit.

But our Lord and the disciples did need some help. They were overworked. They spent all day preaching and teaching and healing the afflicted, and then they had to be back to camp to clean up, get groceries, prepare the supper, and wade through other humdrum tasks. It was too much. Mary suggested that Mary of Magdela round up some women who were free to take care of all those domestic chores. We called ourselves the "seven women." I guess you could say we were the first community of sisters-religious. Mary Magdalene was not very practical. She was the "cheerer-upper" of the group. As moral support for us all, she was the backbone (and the funny bone) of our existence. Joanna was the administrator; she had connections all over the place. Because of her husband's position, she had clout. We called her "Scrounger" when we felt like being silly. If anything was needed, she got it. If there was a bargain to be had, she knew of it.

I was in charge of the meals and I decided where to pitch our tents. The other four were a big help. There was strong Leah, Andrew's daughter, who would carry water on her shoulders for miles. There were the twins, the two oldest daughters of Jairus. (They were so happy about their kid sister being raised from the dead, they wanted to join our job corps.) Finally, there was Rebecca, my niece. I think she joined us because she was attracted to the apostle John. That didn't work out, and she married Matthias soon after Easter. She was a blessing to me those 14 months we were together. We always worked in the kitchen. We knew each other's thoughts.

We were a mobile unit, moving as the Lord directed us. It was good work, and hard, too. The disciples knew that they could relax when they got back home. It was such a happy time. The men would help clean up after supper. Then we would sit around the fire, the cooking coals made brighter by the cedar logs, and we'd talk over the day we spent. Jesus would explain why he acted as he did. He linked that day's teaching with what he said on other occasions. The apostles reported their adventures, asked questions, got their orders for the next day. The women had their story time as well. We also announced the menu for the next day. (There was much teasing about that, especially from Philip and Andrew; Philip because he was a natural comedian; Andrew because he pretended that Leah and the other three were still his "little girls.")

Each evening would end with a gentle time for prayer. Jesus would begin it. I shall treasure those moments always, and everyone who wanted to would have a chance to start our periods of silence with words of wonder about God's gifts.

I was content to be an ordinary housewife adapting to a different style of house. It was such a surprise when I found out that I was made special by the disciples after Pentecost. They didn't single me out exactly. I was also mentioned after Mary Magdelene and Joanna...but I was mentioned. In Luke's story of the Lord's sojourns through Judea, my name was put right in there.

I was a somebody after all. That's just what I want to be, Father, for all the self-styled drudges in the world. With my new nickname, Justa, I will invest a gentle dignity in all those who prefix their job descriptions with "just a": just a stevedore, just a housewife, just a volunteer, just a secretary, just a trucker or farmhand or whatever, just a second-string ballplayer who plugs in where needed, just a chorus member, just one of the family who comes in handy for the chores, just an assembly line worker, and (worst of all) just a loser.

I will give them your compassion, Father, not pity. Nowhere is the difference between compassion and pity so clearly marked as in this category. They are infected with too much self-pity as it is. Any pity from me would only make them wallow deeper in their degradation.

That's the trouble with good people who do their good work in the background. Whenever they start checking the time clock of service, they always judge their devotion to be over-dutiful, and everyone else, by comparison, falls short. Then they feel sorry for themselves and are tempted to quit on life, turning to real non-entities by drinking or taking drugs or pigging out on food, or just plain pouting.

So I won't give them pity. That is their poison. I'll give them harmony. I'll lead them to the insight that they have their innate dignity because you love them, Father, for who they are, not just for what they do. I will stretch the dimensions of their self-appraisal so that they can see the full range of their daily routine, not just the drudgery of it. They will understand the inter-dependence of it all as I did when I realized how many people we seven women were helping because we gave Jesus and the apostles those longer afternoons to do their ministry in peace without worrying about what's for supper.

Compassion will be theirs for the asking. And with it will come a new zest for life, a revalued enthusiasm for the well-being of others, and a good feeling of their place in their world.

Let me begin this ministry, Father. If I can enkindle enthusiasm in just one member of the family, one employee on the job, one nurse on the hospital floor, one nun in the motherhouse, one any-body in a group of self-styled nobodies, these individuals in their newly-found exuberance will influence the rest. Then routine chores will become charismatic opportunities, drudgery will be the raw material of dignity and no one will be "just a" any more.

Jesus Speaks

Yes, Father, let my dear, dear friend be commissioned for this work. It's too bad she cannot personally appear on Earth. I'll never forget how Susanna could turn leftovers into delicious meals. We all looked forward to going home. The women saw to it that everything was as comfortable and as relaxed as it could be. But of course she can't return, and we won't supervise the cooking for bored housewives and directly inject excitement into anybody's dull routine. But Justa can be a good influence, healing some of the emotional drain of humdrum existence. She will give all dejected people a shot of dignity and the promise of a place of honor among us. She will give them the consolation that comes when people take the time to feel our divine support.

God Speaks

Yes. By all means, yes. I like the plan. I call it good, just as I called the world good when I first let earth breathe life.

I'd like to add a little footnote. It delighted me when you described Mary Magdelene as the backbone and the funnybone of your little company. She was often caught up in depression. Yet it frequently happens that the depressed and the disillusioned can be the best ones to cheer others up. (Clowns and comics are seldom funny to themselves.) But with balance in their souls, they become the best antidote to others who are down, the best healers of the depressed.

And so with you, Susanna...pardon me...Justa. You can be the best antidote to those who feel dejected, or relegated as a nobody. They have injected themselves with this characterization. We don't think they are nobodies. That was why I made sure St. Luke placed your name in the gospel— to give hope and enthusiasm to all the team players of the world. Once these people realize their dignity, they can, in turn, help others claim their places of honor and live with more enthusiasm.

Let us pray for this success. Please, everybody, say "Amen."

(And so they do.)

THE STORY OF

The Supervisor

JOANNA, ANOTHER OF THE PROVIDERS

With Jesus were the twelve apostles and certain women who had been cured of evil spirit and infirmities—Mary who is called the Magdelene, from whom seven devils had gone out; and Joanna, the wife of Chusa, Herod's steward; and Susanna; and many others who used to provide for them out of their means.   Luke 8:1-3

Joanna Speaks
Good Father, Susanna has brought up my name. Let me enter my candidacy to show your compassion to the people in my area.

I would like to be known as the "Supervisor." That was my calling and my character on Earth. I don't want to be called Joanna, wife of Chusa, who was second in authority to King Herod. (Although that was my name and rank.) I loved my husband then, as I do now, but I don't want to help my Care People as the wife of a big shot.

The name "Supervisor" points to the people I will direct my concern to. I had a good head on my shoulders and enjoyed managerial and political power. I know the hazards of this lifestyle, as well as its joys. I certainly don't want to be known as the "Scrounger." That was acceptable during that year or so when we women helped Jesus and his disciples. I rather enjoyed the nickname, then. It made me feel at home—a well-functioning member of a team, not just an authority figure. Susanna considered herself a "nobody" for a long time; I was always a "somebody." Even as a child, I smoothed the way for my friends. I helped them with their studies, broke the ice at parties so that boys and girls could shed their shyness and get together...things like that. And when I married Chusa, it was the catch of the season. He was bound for greatness, thanks to his connections, wit, and urbanity. Together, we soon reached high positions in our world. In today's language, the chief steward would be called the "Executive Vice President."

We were a team, Chusa and I. Of course, he had the name. I was, legally, only his wife, in a man's world. But in effect, we were partners in policy. I had as much influence on the politics of that country as had King Solomon's mother in her time.

We prospered, Chusa and I. Then Jesus arrived on the scene, very challenging, masterful, logical, and inspiring. I could see he was a born leader. (It takes one to know one.) We talked privately many times. I pledged him my support, and I didn't hide my allegiance. Those Pharisees—with their threats of exclusion—were not powerful enough to touch us. Chusa and I were above their petty tyranny.

I promised to help Jesus in any way I could. Soon, he took me up on it. He was forming a group of women who would take care of the needs of the disciples—to free them to work with the people. Of course, Jesus never asked for money; that might hinder his ministry. He and his followers were most willing to live in a state of poverty. No frills, but they had to have the necessities of life. Staples such as food, tents, eating utensils, and bed-rolls didn't drop out of the skies.

That's where I came in. Many merchants and grocers owed me favors. (This was for favors I did for them in court.) I could drive bargains with them, and, yes, I did scrounge many things for free.

That year was the most beautiful and fulfilling time I ever spent. I was a kind of commuter. During the day, I left the women to do the shopping for supplies. At night, I would return to be one of the faces around the campfire—listening to Jesus, sharing stories and good humor with the men, planning the next day's venture with the women, praying together...treasuring each moment. The weekends I went home to my husband and family. They needed me, too. I found that I could do as much work at home— in two short days—as used to engage me for a week.

Then came the gathering storm of enmity. Scribes and Pharisees joined ranks with the Sanhedrin and the court of Herod. Everybody could see a clash coming. The ordinary people were still on our side. I expected (just like all the disciples) that Jesus would finally display his power and lead a revolt. But he didn't. He disbanded our group, told us to go home. He must suffer and die for all people...and he must do it alone. I was crushed; we all were. I felt the way high management supervisors feel when Wall Street crashes, or when business takes a sudden downslide. Jesus, so powerful to accomplish good, so perfectly in command of all circumstances, let himself be crucified.

We all were devastated that day we now call Good Friday. Chusa and I contributed our stock of ointment for the burial. We welcomed Mary as she joined us, back from Calvary. No words were spoken, only gestures. Arms clasped in a hug so that shoulders caught tears; hands gently patting the backs of hunched-up bodies. But there were no speeches; there was no hope. Mary helped us wait out the silence of the next two days.

Then came the news. It filtered slowly into our disbelief. When Jesus entered, he came right through the locked doors of our fears...like a ghost. We thought he was a ghost, a figment of our wishful thinking, an apparition giving shallow substance to our hope that we could return to the good old days. But then Jesus took a piece of fish from the stove and started to eat it, right in front of us...with eyes enjoying our stunned looks of wonder. Then he put us all at ease. He explained the Scriptures, reminding us of what he had told us over and over (the part we never wanted to listen to!), expounding the whole plan of love that began so many centuries ago.

You all know the rest. The Acts of the Apostles records how the first community of believers came to be. I was, as usual, assigned to be supervisor of all the necessary logistics. It was good. We lived happy lives there; and now, in heaven, we live even more happily.

I've mentioned, mostly, only the bright spots of my story. But there was the bad side of me. At Herod's court, I sometimes used my power for self-serving ends. I wasn't always patient with those who were not as logical or as efficient as I. And even during those lovely months with Jesus and the disciples, I had many perilous bouts with depression. Sometimes I gave in to them. All humans think, at times, "I'm giving to others more than I'm getting back!" I wondered about this. I doubted the fairness of it all. Sometimes a little voice inside me fretted, "Are people just using me? Is it worth it to use my managerial skills while those who work under me express jealousy behind my back?" I even asked myself if the nickname "Scrounger" was said all in fun—or did it have a bite to it? It's hard to give orders and think about what is fair for everyone...and at the same time not get enough support yourself.

I'm not complaining, Father. I just want to say that I know the emotional pitfalls of people in high places. Since I was one of them, I can help them better. They sorely need the kindness Jesus gave us on Easter Sunday when his eyes danced with joy, and his mercy was so tangible and his love so obvious and real.

Compassion is a virtue that many authority figures find hard to deal with. It is confused sometimes with softness, and feared as a hindrance to progress. It registers emotion, which can cause a lack of energy, a slipshod effort.

But compassion is the only virtue that can put humanity into one's plans and a good heart into any drive for excellence. Compassion is part of your larger plan of love, Father. And only love can be the mainstay of achievements, no matter what they are.

Let me try to put first things first, then. Harshness of temper will be softened. Jealousies at work, and all that contemptible infighting among the powerful, will be eradicated. Great deeds will take longer to complete...but they will last longer, because everyone will find dignity in the effort. And most of all, love will be better understood.

Jesus Speaks

Yes, Joanna, I did enjoy your story. I'm not sure how my eyes were dancing. I'll have to check that out in a mirror, to see if I can still do it. But I do know the joy that was in my heart. That left-over piece of fish (which had cooled off on top of the stove) was the tastiest morsel I ever ate—because of the joy it brought to all my friends.

Father, the name "Supervisor" is just right for Joanna. She managed very well whatever responsibility I assigned to her. She is also a "super-visor" in the sense that she saw things in ways that were superior to most. That is still her gift. It is also the special talent of all good managers everywhere. She was aware of the larger view of things: the preparations needed; the possible consequences that would proceed; the motivation required for all personnel, in order to act together...everything. She was born with these gifts. But it was our compassion that gave inner vision to her super-vision. Now she will do the same for others.

God Speaks

Yes, Joanna, Supervisor, begin. We will be with you. I ask you to select a number of saints to help you, those who died after they retired from prominent positions.

These men and women who have retired used to wield great power, and enjoyed honors and privileges. Their work meant so much to them that they didn't prepare too well for their later years. Now they often feel cast off because their work-world is gone. They need our compassion, some of them desperately. Work it out together. Do what you can to help them dignify their aging years and retain a sense of their past achievements.

If anyone can do this, you can, good Joanna.

And the citizens of heaven say, "Amen."

17 Following the Crowd

THE STORY OF

Groupee

ONE OF THE DAUGHTERS OF JERUSALEM

As they led Jesus away [to be crucified] there were some women who were wailing and lamenting him. But Jesus, turning to them, said, "Daughters of Jerusalem, do not weep for me; but weep for yourselves and for your children. But behold, days are coming in which [you] will say to the mountains, 'Fall on us' and to the hills, 'Cover us!' For if in the case of green wood they do these things, what is to happen in the case of the dry?"   Luke 23:27-32

Groupee Speaks

Good Father, let me speak in the name of my longstanding friends, the daughters of Jerusalem. Together, we will work on behalf of all those people who are so attached to a group that they assume their personality.

That's not bad—not necessarily. I want to be called "Groupee" because I'm proud of it. The close bond I felt with my friends was one of the causes for my being here, in heaven. Some people are independent, walking to the beat of their own drum; because of circumstances, special talents, or inventive minds, they choose the more demanding life of going it alone. Many others (like me) are content to enjoy holidays, endure hardships, live out their ordinary lives by holding hands with a huddle of friends...much as children hold each other's hands when they visit a museum.

Of course, these categories are relative. Nobody is completely independent. There are no absolute solitares, no matter how original the mind may be. And we Groupees are not abject slaves to the corporate personality. We have our own ideas. (And we guard them.) We work and play together because each member recognizes unique gifts in the others.

But for the most part, my friends in the association thought the same way, shared the same interests, reacted to good and evil with the same battery of responses...and were conditioned by shared schooling and social strata.

We were friends for a long time. Whenever the Rabbi wanted to give a bazaar, he knew he could count on us. Whenever there was a disaster— like a fire that destroyed a home or Herod's soldiers massacring infant children—we were the first on the scene to give all the care and consolation possible. We did a lot of good for others; and it was effective because of our consolidated effort.

Of course, there was the bad side of all of this. We gossiped. I suppose that's the occupational hazard of all groups who do good. We were very hard on people who weren't like us. We found it difficult to experiment with new ideas, new ways of doing things; we liked the old ways better. And we tended to be preoccupied with what was wrong with the world. The emphasis was on the negative. One would bring up news about an accident at work, and everybody would go on about the hazards of the work place. Somebody was ailing on death's door...and in no time there was news of a hundred sickbeds.

In particular (and this ultimately involved us in the gospel) we tended to dwell on what was wrong with the politics of our world: the occupation army, our own greedy authorities conspiring with Rome,, outrageous taxes, corruption in high places, reckless youth. You name it, we knew what was wrong with it! Once we got going, anyone could enter our group in high spirits and become downcast in no time at all.

Our subject under discussion—the Friday morning that put us into the gospel—was the brutality of Pilate's commandos, the wickedness of the Sanhedrin, and the unspeakable lust for blood demonstrated by the mob at the Praetorium. We were against capital punishment in principle; but now, here was a man—Jesus of Nazareth—who was absolutely undeserving of his death. He was a good man: that was the word from all our sources of information. He healed the sick and gave sight to the blind and taught about love. The authorities claimed he was an imposter. He taught dangerous heresy, they said. He pretended to be the Messiah, but lacked the proper credentials and didn't go through proper channels.

We didn't go into this Messiah controversy; theology wasn't our thing. If he was wrong in his teaching, why didn't they just deport him? Or silence him in a court of law? Why kill him? Why did they hate the man so much as to stir up the people so that Pilate was forced to have him scourged and mocked?

We decided to do something. We'd form a demonstration— half-way up the road to Golgotha. We would publicly protest against injustice, and against this act of wickedness in particular. We were already caught up in a frenzy of grief. Then, when we actually saw Jesus stumbling under his burden, his face all bloody from the crown of thorns, his clothes all torn from the times he fell... he was so pitiable a sight, we sobbed convulsively and cried out in grief. We could not contain our deep sorrow.

Then Jesus stopped. We marveled that he was even strong enough to speak, he was so battered. He switched everything around: We wanted to pity him, and thought he would be consoled as we ventilated our complaints against those responsible for such an atrocity.

But Jesus turned things around. He did not want to enter the mood of our protest against evil. Imagine that! We were expressing our outrage against the evil others had done to him, and he was preaching to us! He told us to remember finalities: the ultimate outcome of life...and after death, then what? He read our souls in one brief instant and told us to correct our own sinfulness, our own selfishness and the neglect of our families because of the time we wasted clucking about the injustices of humankind.

"Well! The nerve of him!" That was our first reaction. Some of our group were so resentful, they changed their tune and almost gleefully followed him up the hill to watch him die. But not all of us did that; I didn't. Our Lord's words hit home. I realized I had been too dependent on the whims and instincts of the group. I left and went to the Pool of Siloam, the healing pool. (No one was there; the crowd had gone to see the crucifixion.) I prayed, there in that quiet place, and gradually came to understand that I had tried to give Jesus my pity and he was giving me compassion.

Yes, I was neglecting my family. I would change that. Yes, I was allowing my preoccupation with what was wrong with the world to occupy most of my waking hours, and as a consequence I had little energy for making the world better. I had never thought about finalities, what would happen after death. Not until that day. What is my purpose in life, I finally asked myself. How will I end up? Is there life after death? Most of our teachers believed there was...but they were vague about it. What will this life be like? How will it happen? How should I prepare for it?

After making some inquiries, I found out that Jesus had talked about heaven as confidently as he talked about God's love. He promised that he would take us there.That's why he was being crucified: for giving such hope to the poor and filling people's minds with outrageous pretensions. But was it outrageous? If what Jesus said was true, everything makes sense, including death itself. If Jesus was false, nothing makes sense...nothing! And my drab life—going on day after day, a "groupee" in the ebb and flow of immediate emotions—my drab life is useless. Indeed, everybody's existence is so pathetic that we all would do well to scream at the hills to fall on us, the mountains to crush us!

As you know, Father, that Good Friday was a very good afternoon for me. The prayer arising from those hours of grace changed me. Not completely, of course. I remained a "Groupee" to the end—but now I was one of another kind. I joined the disciples after Easter. I was a successful convincer. Many converts came over to our way because of what I said to them. I always had a knack for working in a group; this came in handy when I talked at church functions and house gatherings.

I want to continue this way, my Father. I will show the same compassion that Jesus showed me when he was on his way to be crucified. With my help, many other socially-orientated individuals will find the right balance to their need for being alone and their need for being with friends. Please give me permission to continue what I started soon after that first Easter.

Jesus Speaks

Thank you for saying the things you said, Leah. (I hope you don't mind my calling you by the name that I remember you by.) Because of what you just said, you have given me more reason to be grateful for the way everything turned out. (I am speaking from the human side of me, of course.) One of the greatest causes of distress—especially during the last few months before my death—was wondering, "Have I really reached people? Has anything I said really rubbed off? Will the apostles finally understand what I am doing...and why? Will anybody's life be changed?" I wondered about these things when I spoke to you and the other daughters of Jerusalem. Yes, I had to really push myself and summon all the energy I had to say those words. But I had to say them. You looked so smug behind your tears, so pleased with yourselves for pitying me. I appreciated the fact that you meant well. But pity was way off the mark. It was victory-over-death that I was bound for. Compassion was what I needed, the compassion of an understanding heart and the willingness to change.

That's why it felt so good when I heard the whole story about what happened to you and to your family after Easter. It still feels good to hear your story told again today. Thank you.

Father, on this happy occasion, and in this roundabout way, I ratify Groupee's appointment. I have every confidence that she will be effective.

God Speaks

Good. You are duly appointed, dear Leah. And if you can live with the name "Groupee," so can we.

You mentioned a number of people unlike yourself, individuals who for one reason or another do not attach themselves to groups. Many other members of this commission will take care of those who feel left out because of poverty, bigotry, or malicious gossip. But we must also show our loving kindness toward those who *choose* to be alone, people who wish to live apart from society.

Please, my daughter, gather the saints who have made this kind of journey through life. Let it be a one-on-one kind of subtle ministry. It will be good to reach them all. We will be with you: the groupees and the geniuses, the socialites, and the solitaires. And our love will reach all people, according to each one's comprehension and compelling desire for this love.

Citizens of heaven, what say we all?

All in heaven say, "Amen."

THE STORY OF

Mrs. Dismal

MOTHER OF THE GOOD THIEF

Now one of those robbers who were crucified with Jesus was abusing him.... But the other rebuked the man and said, "Do you not even fear God, seeing that you are under the same sentence? We are sentenced justly for we are receiving what our deeds deserved, but this man has done no wrong." And he said to Jesus, "Lord, remember me when you come into your kingdom." And Jesus said to him, "Amen I say to you, this day you shall be with me in paradise."

Luke 23:40-43

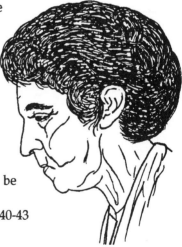

Mrs. Dismal Speaks
Good Father, please call me Mrs. Dismal for this occasion. The ones who will be my special concern for your compassion will be the dismal ones, especially the mothers and fathers who lay guilt

upon themselves because, as they put it, "One of our children has turned out bad!"

The name Mrs. Dismal is right to the point. There has been enough confusion about the names in my story; it would be good to set the record straight. My son has been called the Good Thief. That's a misnomer. When he was a thief, he was no good at all. When he was good, he was no longer a thief. It's only for the last half-hour of his life that we call him good. And besides, the word "thief" is wrong. He was much more than a simple cutpurse. He was a villain of the worst sort: terrorism, murder for hire, kidnapping...you name it.

My son is also called St. Dismas, but that is the Greek word for "being on the right side of Jesus." Of course, my son was not Greek and I never did like the name; imagine, calling a person as though he were just somebody on a map—like calling him Southwest or Ten Miles Farther.

Actually, his name was Ismael. Even at his painful birth, he seemed to be a tragic figure. We called him Ismael, but that name didn't stick. Everybody but his father and I called him The Fox; that's what he was, as soon as he was old enough to run. He was selfish, wary of human tenderness, rapacious, cruel, unmanageable. He was a fox with the girls, too, at an unbelievably young age.

We tried to bring him up right, the fifth of our twelve children. We trained him no differently than the others, but it was useless. Enrolled in the best synagogue for schooling, he either played truant or disrupted the class. We invested in a tutor who was regarded as a strict disciplinarian, but our son broke his jaw. Then he ran away—at 15!—and joined a band of marauders. They started off with different acts of mischief, just for the sport of it. Then they went into acts of meanness, for the cruelty of it. Finally it was terrorism, kidnapping, and murder, for the money they could get from it.

We hid from our neighbors, because we were so ashamed. Our other children, especially the seven younger ones, became like orphans in our care. My husband was depressed, too, but he was realistic: Life must go on. I was much worse; I refused to let life go on. Our boy's scandalous behavior drained me of all my energy. I didn't feel like living any more. I was sure God was doing this to punish me. But where did I go wrong? I tried to bring Ismael up right. I plagued my memory with a re-hash of every step he took, every day of his upbringing, to find flaws in our parental direction.

I wasted away. My children didn't dare chide me, but I could see that they were avoiding my company. Who wants to be around a sour-faced mother who keeps wringing her hands and sobbing her heart out and plods on with the dismal quest for an answer to "What went wrong?"

I had a right to be miserable, and I stuck fast to it! It never occurred to me that my other children had rights, too. And my husband. They forfeited their higher claim to have a good mother and good wife who could love them. But the fact that I neglected them did not bother me a bit. The only thing the rest of my family did was to feed my flames of guilt even more. When I thought about how I was losing their affection, this brought me to an unavoidable conclusion: "See—I'm no good for anybody!"

This lasted many years. My son was about Christ's age when he was caught and sentenced to death. I didn't go to the crucifixion. I couldn't. That would be the last nail in the coffin I made for myself. Maybe I would die soon. I hoped so. For the last few months before Ismael's crucifixion, I had talked a lot about death. It would be such a relief to finish off my misery. Two of my children got up the nerve to argue with me about death being the end of everything. They had heard Jesus of Nazareth speak most convincingly about the afterlife.

O yes, I was brought up piously. I knew the faith of the Macabees' mother and all those heroic people who trusted that they would live with God when this life was over. But these prospects were very vague. Prophets seem to disagree about whether or not we would have life—and what kind of shadow existence it would amount to. I dismissed the whole notion. I'd rather think of death as the blissful end of all my crushed hopes, and nothing more.

But Jesus made me think. He was so certain of that kingdom of heaven, as he called it. And it would not be a shadow existence, he said. It will be so full of life and joy that, by comparison, this world is the real shadow existence. In that place, I would find the end of tears, not the end of life.

I see, now, that heaven is all our Lord had promised. Even more so. But I had my doubts when I went to the East Portico of the Temple to listen to him myself. He pierced my heart when he warned that we must forgive all wrongs, if we are to make it to the place he was preparing. That meant I must forgive myself. Long before, I had already forgiven my son. I blamed myself for all his waywardness, but now I had to let go of the morose moodiness by which I had condemned myself. It was very painful to do so.

My daughters then told me about my son's good death on a cross. They were there, close enough to hear him speak. He did not have his customary leer on his face or anger in his words; no "foxiness." He was a changed man. He even talked about justice and for the first time in his life admitted he was wrong! And then he turned to Jesus...and he prayed—I think that was a first, too—there was love in his heart. He died well.

I am still in awe about how it all worked out in the end. Imagine! Thousands of men and women have been canonized as saints. Millions of millions unmentioned ones are here with us in heaven, but my son—my worrisome, trouble-prone failure of a son—is the only one who was ever canonized by the Lord himself, before he took his last breath!

So you see, Father, my story has a built-in sermon for all the worriers of the world. I want to include more than mothers and fathers with my circle of compassion. There are teachers and coaches and counsellors who are hurting from their apparent failure to change errant behavior in those who seem determined to stay on their self-destructive course. Those who want so much to help can get very discouraged now and then, because no matter what they do or what they say—or how they try, or how long they pray—nothing seems to change.

They need to understand your kindness, Father. First of all, they need to rethink the cruel kindness of your gift of freedom. It seems cruel that you refuse to sabotage free will. People who care so deeply want you to force the prodigals to change their ways, straighten our their lives, start to behave themselves.

Of course you love them. And you want your love to reach them. You show them Jesus from his cross, thirsting for them. You hope that—in the last half hour of their lives—they will turn to the Lord and be their honest selves...that they will end up like my dearest son, my Ismael.

I want them all to learn about real love. With my sympathy, founded upon my bitter-long experience, I can help them understand and accept the fullness of your compassion: its respect for freedom, its patience, and its everlasting promise given to every "problem child" when Jesus gave it to my son. Once they learn your lovestyle, Father, they will be able to love themselves again; and have more energy to care for other people in their lives: those they've been ignoring because of their deep guilt.

Please let me begin, Good Father. The people who care for others—with the anxiety that comes from caring for others—have suffered long enough. And those close to them have also suffered. I will help them, if only they will let me tell them about my Ismael...and the wonderful last half-hour of his life.

Jesus Speaks
Yes, it is just as Mrs. Dismal says; they have suffered long enough. Needlessly so.

As my friend was talking, I was thinking about ecology. The peopled earth is discovering new interest in the environment these days. Ecology is in. Don't waste energy is a big slogan. That's great. We are all for it. But I do wish people would extend their awareness to include spiritual ecology, as well. And nowhere is this more needed than in the tortured hearts of those who worry over others. We want them to pray. We want them to continue all their attempts at behavior modification. But we don't want them to waste so much time and energy over lost causes. By pining away like this, there is nothing left for their other children, the other clients or spouses or friends who have become blocked off.

Let her begin, Father. Her Ismael, who is with us in paradise, will help his mother focus on the energy-wasters of the world. He has a debt he wants to pay to other mothers for the bad time that he gave his own. Together they will give patience to those who have let the sense of guilt deflate them. The need is great. Let our Good Friday compassion, Father, find a place in the hearts of those who wait for it to happen.

God Speaks

Yes, Mrs. Dismal, you will need more help. It is enough responsibility for you to concentrate on the primary task: those who feel guilty or frustrated because they cannot change for the better someone they love.

We are also concerned for those who are indirectly affected. I remember how Ismael's brothers and sisters suffered from what amounted to their mother's abdication. She retired into her misery and they were stuck with the consequences of it all. I want a group of saints—young ones—to make my compassion felt to all who are wronged because of the by-products of self-pity. They need to learn endurance, too. They need to know that somebody loves them, even though they feel neglected.

Oh, how I wish the world were not so sick with sadnesses! I wish wrongs could be righted sooner than they usually are. I wish the good thieves would change before the last half-hour of their lives. But I can only love them—on the sideline of their free will— just like everyone else.

Do what you can, mother of Ismael. We will be with you. The choirs of angels pray in silence for a half-hour.

19 Handling Let-Downs

Devastator Later

MARY OF CLEOPAS

Now there were standing by the cross of Jesus: his mother and his mother's sister, Mary of Cleopas.   John 19:25

[On Easter Sunday afternoon] two of the disciples were going to a village named Emmaus...and while they were conversing and arguing together, Jesus drew near and went along with them. But their eyes were held, so that they could not recognize him. Then Jesus said to them, "What words are you exchanging as you walk, *and are sad?*" Then one of them, named Cleopas, said to him, "Are you the only stranger in Jerusalem who does not know...about Jesus of Nazareth? We were hoping that it was he who would redeem Israel... but he was delivered up to be crucified. And this is the third day since...." Then Jesus said to them, "O foolish ones and slow of heart to believe....Did you not know that the Christ had to suffer these things before entering his glory?" And they drew near the village to which they were going. Jesus acted as though he were going on, but they urged him, saying, "Stay with us...."   Luke 24:13-32, italics added

Devastator Later Speaks
Good Father, I just thought up a good name for my part in your

new compassion program. It's a little fancy, maybe. Many people will be confused by it, but those whose life's history is similar to mine will know immediately what the nickname means.

The people I speak of—those blessed (and burdened) with a slow fuse capacity in times of crisis—are in the minority. Even so, there are thousands of people like me, and they need a long compassionate chat with Jesus, just as I did.

We are heros at crunch time. We act decisively when we have to. We work at picking up the pieces after a tragedy, when other people are coming apart. We are resolute in our loving care, firm in making prudent decisions, alert at keeping everybody else away from drowning in despair. Our courage and efficiency is the stuff that keeps others going. We are the ones they make medals of honor for. We are the names recalled in sagas and folklore. We are the glue that keeps a family together in catastrophe. We remain cool in the bedlam of heated passion.

So far, so good. In the thick of chaos, we do our work well. But then comes afterwards...that's when we heroic figures crumble. Because we saw more than the others did when it was time for action, we also see more of the dire consequences, once the storm has passed.

That's how it was with me. On Good Friday afternoon, I was a pillar of strength for all concerned. My husband was useless... hiding his sobs and his fear behind his protective cloak. I don't mind seeing a man cry, but I hate to hear him whimper. Cleopas was doing just that. St. John was strong enough, but his silence was more of a dazed shrug that vaguely agreed to things he didn't completely understand. He didn't faint, or anything like that. He obeyed the Lord's command to take Mary to be his mother. But, for the most part, he was emotionally immobilized.

Mary, though, was strong. She was most heroic, and compliant to her son's last wish. But her sorrow was heavy. Her heart was so full of God's mysterious love that she could not think of practical matters, such as, "Once the Sabbath darkness comes, then what do we do, where do we go?" The other women who were on Calvary were like sheep without a shepherd.

I took charge. I gave John's arm to Mary and whispered some

advice to the other women. Then I led the procession down the ravine and over to the upper room.

For almost two sleepless days and nights, our lives were a waiting hell! Nobody did much. Mostly, we looked down at our sandals. I prepared the broth and baked the bread. I had to practically force food down their throats. It was a terrible ordeal.

Somehow we made it. When the third day dawned, Cleopas and I had to leave. Relatives were expecting us. After we said goodbye, I just caved in. All my adrenalin had drained away. After cheering up everybody else and feeding them and telling them to be patient, I had no words of comfort left for myself. My hope was buried in the tomb. I had counted on Jesus to be the Messiah of our people, but three days passed and nothing happened. Gloom. Listlessness. Despair.

Cleopas started arguing with me. He took the words I had previously said to others and threw them back at me. I couldn't stand his lecturing me with my own speeches. I wanted to stuff his mouth with a wet rag. Didn't he understand that everything was over? That Jesus refused to use his power? That he turned out to be an imposter after all?

I was winning the argument. Then, suddenly, a stranger joined us. I didn't even see him well, because my eyes were swollen with tears and pent-up rage. He was just somebody else for me to turn on besides my husband. I told him the whole sad story of my sawdust hopes and my now-jilted love for Jesus.

The stranger turned on me. On us, really, but I got the brunt of his reproach. He called up all the prophets—their words and their own suffering. He skipped over the champions of victory, like David and Solomon and Judith, the people I had linked to Jesus. I wanted the Messiah to be a hero of heroes, the most powerful politico in the whole world, the banner-waving king of peace. Instead, he talked about the humbled heroes of our history: the martyred Isaiah, the broken Jeremiah, the suffering servant who would not dictate the rules of peace, but modestly plant the seeds of love… and be condemned by wicked men because he did.

Then the stranger talked about the just man rising from death, and about the place in heaven he was preparing for all. Indeed, he spoke the same way Jesus did. Only this time I really heard his words. I always admired, even worshipped, Jesus. But before this day, I had painted his unvarnished words with my own wishes for a powerful Messiah, who would be undaunted by adversity and impervious to any strategies the forces of evil might devise. The whole world knows what happened next, how we were fed with the bread of life. We then retraced our steps. The energy I displayed on Calvary came back to me. Three days earlier my instincts guessed what God could do to bring a good ending out of the chaos of defeat. Now I knew that these instincts were correct.

That's my story: the good, then the bad, then the good of it.

Cleopas and I can help those who do great work when the pressure is on, and then collapse when the work is over. I want them to understand that everything doesn't depend on them. They should rest up after their arduous demands, whatever they may have been. Let them rest easy, not sit tight on the edge of their chairs, still shadow-boxing enemies who aren't there. I will help them as their strength returns. And I will take them back to the times when they were at their best, when their good instincts and amazing energy and fast thinking saved the day.

Good Father, they need the same toning down and tuning up that Jesus gave me. They need compassion when the tide is turned and hopes collapse and plans, so well begun, get frustrated. Help me to help them see that suffering is so much a part of all worthwhile projects. Patience, too. We want their gifts to continue, their nobility and courage to stay on course, no matter what the vicissitudes may be. We want them to finish their lives gloriously, with us in heaven. They want—and they need, as soon as possible—our compassionate understanding and our patient wisdom.

Jesus Speaks

Yes, I have seen it happen so many times. Every one of my saints has a story similar to Devastator Later. Martyrs speak of suffering most eloquently. Mystics know well the sufferings of their dark nights, their feelings of abandonment, uselessness, and dryness. They also know that the quality of life that returned to them after their purging was less selfish than before, more docile to our teaching.

That is how it was with Cleopas and his wife. They wanted control, so they tried to put me in their pocket. I had determined on a course of love, and they had to empty their pockets, so to speak. That caused pain, but thanks to the emptying, they were better than before.

Everyone experiences turning points as my friends of Emmaus did. Others feel it more strongly. Compassion is what they need from us, the quiet kind. We cannot change their world the way they wish. If we did, they would never grow. They would be possessed by their own pretensions. No, we must let them grope in darkness for the patience they need. When they become aware of love's priority, they will manage all things well.

If they read my Scriptures—and know the purpose of my crucifixion—they will be comforted by the stories of great men and women who know why suffering is always linked with love. My good friend, Devastator Later, will be their guide.

God Speaks

Yes, Mary, yours is an important responsibility. The gifted individuals who are "devastated later" will find you there to comfort and support them.

Cleopas, I want you to concentrate on the other people who surround all those high-voltage individuals, like satellites, in whatever arena they make their leadership felt: in politics, big business, academia, sports, theater, military commands. Don't overlook those who, like your wife, take charge of things in a family crisis.

Assigned to these prominent personalities are people like yourself. Let us call them the "backdrop people"— spouses, children, assistants, those behind the scenes who give support...and sometimes have to pick up the pieces when the action is over.

Help them, Cleopas. Let them know my compassion. They are so used to giving comfort to the more talented, they often get depressed because nobody is comforting them. We understand. We feel for them. My Son will nourish their unnoticed heroism by his support. They will receive this comfort and compassion "at the breaking of the bread."

The citizens of heaven say, "Well said, my Lord, My God. Amen. Amen."

20 Being Patient with Those Less Talented

Young Reliable

TABITHA, CALLED DORCAS, GAZELLE

At Joppa there was a certain disciple named Tabitha [which is translated Dorcas, or Gazelle]. This woman had devoted herself to good works and acts of charity. But...she fell ill...and died. Then two disciples said to Peter, "Come to us without delay." And Peter arose...and on his arrival, they took him to the upper room. All the women stood about him weeping and showing him the the tunics and cloaks Dorcas used to make for them. [Then] Peter...turning to the body said, "Tabitha, arise!" She opened her eyes....Then Peter gave her his hand and raised her up....Then he gave her back to her people alive. Acts 9: 36-42

Jesus said, "To what shall I compare the [people] of this generation? What are they like? They are like children sitting in the marketplace and calling to one another: 'We piped a tune to you, but you did not dance; we wailed a dirge, but you did not weep!' For John the Baptist has come, neither eating bread nor drinking wine, and you say, 'He is [a fanatic with a] demon within!' Then I come, *enjoying life,* and you say, 'Behold a glutton and a drunkard, a friend of tax collectors and sinners!' O well...." Luke 7:31-35 (The phrase in italics, Kleist translation)

Young Reliable Speaks

Good Father, put me in a young time frame. I want to focus on the gifted and good-looking who are in their teens and twenties and excel in leadership among their peers because of their attractiveness or because of the ease with which they achieve things. They are "class," the ones that others rely on.

They need your compassion, Father. First of all, they need it so that they can love others a little more modestly. If they do not love, their talents can turn into haughtiness, and then they become more and more bossy and irritable. It is so tempting for them to judge others by the standard of their own competence. They need to know the meekness of your Son, who even though he was gifted with absolute excellence, made himself available to all the "little ones." Once they are grafted to grace, they will think more about "How can I help others, as one of them?" They will think less about "Why can't they be like me and see it my way?" That is the compassion they need. Genuine love must suffer if it wants to serve.

But they also need another kind of mercy, for their own support. Superiority in any form can cause alienation. Very often they can feel alone...even in the middle of activity, and they are sometimes ostracized because of their giftedness. If they are beautiful, others are jealous. If they are competent, friends, co-workers, and family can take them for granted and rely on them too much. They then often wonder, "Yes, I give myself to others, but who really cares about me?"

That's where we come in, Good Father: to show them that we care and that we understand their particular brand of loneliness that sometimes causes tears.

You know how it was with me. In my childhood, teens, and twenties, I struggled with the good and the bad of my giftedness. People nicknamed me Gazelle, the beautiful and graceful one. I was that, all right. I charmed adults into granting us children special favors. I excelled in school and led the games at playtime. It was this ability that was featured in the background of a gospel scene. I was the eight-year-old heroine who "explained" Christ's exasperation with the Pharisees.

Peter told me all about it. It was one of those hot summer days. when nobody felt like moving. Jesus was fourteen years old at the time, on a vacation with his family at the home of Joseph's uncle. They had hoped to relax there, with the cool Mediterranean breeze to fan them. No breeze that day. Nothing. I was bored to death. I tried to get a little life into my friends. I danced and clapped and swayed around, and I tried to get my playmates to dance with me. Nothing doing! So, I started to mimic their long faces and get them to laugh at themselves; and I sang a dirge over them as if to mourn for them because they all seemed to be so sad. That didn't work either. Nothing could amuse them. That's when I lost my temper. (My irritation and impatience displayed that bad side of my character, even way back then. When leaders don't get cooperation, they often get testy!)

Well, Jesus was watching this whole performance, half-hidden in the shade nearby. Apparently, Peter told me, it made a big impression on him, for he remembered it sixteen years later. At that time, he was getting more and more frustrated with the sullenness of the scribes and the Pharisees, who were deliberately blocking God's appeals by saying negative things against John the Baptist and then against Jesus himself. One day Jesus was very, very angry, but he gentled his wrath by expressing it indirectly. I became his parable, so that the Pharisees could think about childish quarrels and see the silliness of their own behavior.

I say this because I was a gospel girl; I want to fit in with all the other gospel women here.

Then I became a teenager. The boys and girls would look to me as their leader. I arranged the socials, picnics, the fun times. I helped them with their homework and their knitting chores. The boys liked me, and some of them—the ones I wanted to—fell in love with me. I was happy, growing up...most of the time. But parents would point to me and say to their daughters, "Why can't you be more like Tabitha?" This made my friends bitter sometimes. And jealous. The boys got mad at me, too, when I showed them up in school...or in games. I sometimes wished I could be more ordinary, more like everyone else. It was tiresome and demanding to have to be the leader all the time. Too many people

relied on me for too many things. I got weary of their expectations. (That's when I'd start scolding.)

When I married, the same pattern continued. O, I liked to do
good; no denying that. I'd feel terrible if I were not making a gar-
ment for this one, baking some cookies for that one, caring for the
families whose mothers were sick. That kind of thing. I was one of
the pillars of Joppa. As I got older, I still had a tendency to want
to control the people I did good for. But those occasions became
less and less frequent.

My real trouble was discouragement. It seemed that everybody
was relying on me, just taking me for granted. "Please do this,
Dorcas," they would say; or "I'm counting on you, Tabitha, to
make sure they all get here!" And then my friends and family
would go their ways, leaving me with all the work. Little cooperation and seldom a word of thanks! I was amazed by the report
of how they praised me in front of Peter. They said how wonderful I was...and what I did for everybody...and how gracious and
good I was...and how awful that I had to die when I was only in
my early thirties.

Well, I'm glad they thought so highly of me. It moved St. Peter
to ask Jesus for the miracle that I be brought back to life. But I
would like to have heard some of this before I died.

So you see, Father, I know the sensitive nature and the de-
pressing self-doubts that can assail those young people whom I
call the "gifted and good-looking." I was one of them. I've experienced pleasures and pitfalls similar to theirs.

That is why I want to be called "Young Reliable" for this commission. Reliable is our main characteristic; we can be relied on, in
all kinds of ways. But so often people like us are referred to as the
"Old Reliable." I know this is partly a compliment. "Old" is meant
to mean trustworthy, comfortable, dependable, like an old pair of
slippers or an old friend. But it also can mean "taken for granted,"
"serviceable but not noteworthy," "useful until used up." The
word in this respect is derogatory. It's just old.

I want "young" to be the forceful adjective as I take on my responsibilities of sharing your compassion, Father. I will concentrate most of my attention on young people. And "young" also

suggests *re*generation, an uplifting surge of energy, the promise of growth that talented youth give the whole world. I want to give everyone the hopeful expectancy that wonders, "What more can I do?"—not the dull throb of disappointment that looks back on the past and mutters, "I did all that, so why don't they appreciate me?"

If you permit me, Father, I will put youth-full-ness back into the youth, and I will place a new surge of self-confidence into the gifts that you have given them.

Jesus Speaks

Yes, indeed. So be it. I could tell, even when I noticed that child of eight in Joppa, that Tabitha was extraordinary. It was easy to see how she would develop into the greatness that became hers. I thought of her not only when I spoke about the child in the playground complaining about the sullenness of friends, but also when I made all those references about the rich getting richer and the poor going broke! I wasn't talking about material capitalism or financial craftiness. I was on a spiritual and psychological plane. I could see it in little children, everywhere.

Some children are kind to others. They are praised for this and relied on. With a kind of early momentum, they grow in virtue. They become "rich" in the development of a lively spirit and outgoing personality. The gifted continue to grow in giftedness, as long as bitterness or self-pity does not block things.

On the other hand, some children seem selfish almost from the very start of their lives. They don't play well with others; they are soured or oversensitive, or they always emphasize what is wrong. They have few friends to start with and even that circle of friends starts to shrink, predictably.

So it is with spiritual gifts, my Father. Teenagers who take our teaching lightly will develop a spirit which will register only the crassest sensibilities. And they will "go broke" soon. I wish, Father, that you would appoint another group of saints who will be able to influence the "less gifted and good looking" so that they will be able to experience our compassion, too.

God Speaks

Yes, my son. Thank you. As usual, you express my thoughts perfectly. I do want to establish a sub-committee for this purpose. Suzanna will chair it since she knows how it feels to be "just one of the group." I want her to enlist teenagers who felt this way too. They will do all they can to reach the less fortunate, those who are so because of handicap, disabilities, unattractiveness, poverty, accident, or some other incapacity. They will show these people how we love them in a special way. Our gentleness is manifested best when we love the poor in every sense of the word.

This new committee—my "agents for youth"—will do their best to entice the underachievers out of the trap of making comparisons, which is their greatest obstacle to growth. Young people can never be happy as long as they keep on wishing they were "as good as" or "as smart as" or "as rich and pretty as" someone else. If they surmount this difficulty, they will be able to throw off that sullen mood displayed by the playmates of Young Reliable—and the very ugly "sourpuss attitude" of the Pharisees that so exasperated my Son.

Once they can relax and be themselves, they will lead good lives. They will become better at operating with their own talents. And we can fill up heaven with more people who have already learned how to be happy while they were on earth.

The youthful spirit of all the saints respond, "Amen."

21 When Your Gifts Go Unappreciated

Ms. Careering

LYDIA OF NORTHERN GREECE

A certain woman named Lydia—a seller of purple [a dry goods merchant] from the city of Thyatira [northern Greece]—was listening to Paul. And the Lord touched her heart and she believed what Paul was saying. And when she and her household had been baptized, she appealed to Paul and Luke, "If you have judged me to be a believer in the Lord, come to my house and stay." And she insisted....

Acts 16:14-15

Ms. Careering Speaks

Good Father, let me speak in behalf of all single women and men whose careers are the most important thing in their lives. They need to experience your Compassion.

While Jesus was preaching in Judea and Galilee, I was making my fortune in the cosmopolitan towns of Greece. It was a good life for me. In a man's world, I had learned to respond with boldness and courage. It was exciting! There were new branch offices to open, new managers to train, problems of supply and personnel to straighten out. My merchandising efforts occupied almost all of my time.

In my career, I did not know much about love. There were always people around me, but these were mostly connected with my work. My household was made up of servants and certain members of my family that I took in. I treated them fairly. They were loyal to me. We had a fine relationship, but I couldn't call them friends. Then Paul and Luke came into my life. They didn't change my world—they changed the way I lived in it. As was my custom, I took my long lunch break beside the river, near my home in Thyratira. It was the only way I could break off from the pressure of decision making. The flow of water in the river calmed me down. I could think there. Away from the bustle of everyday affairs, I could reflect upon more ongoing enterprises. And I could consider other aspects of my life, such as philosophy. (I had been taking night courses in the Great Thinkers. Plato stirred me to consider death and the possibility of life after death. Aristotle challenged me to wonder about God and the fundamental characteristics of love and friendship.)

One warm June afternoon, by my favorite bend in the river, I was thinking about God and the afterlife and about love and friendship. Suddenly Paul's strong voice barged in upon my peace. I was almost a quarter-mile away, but thanks to his strident voice and the down-river breeze, I heard him as though he were right next to me. And more than "next to me"! He seemed to be talking *inside* of me. Everything "clicked" almost at once. My questions about life—the purpose of my life–settled down within me. It was the same good feeling I had when I balanced the books for the year. Jesus was the key that put all my thoughts and wonderments together. I wanted to know more about the kind of love that would prompt someone to die for others. I wanted to pursue the concept of afterlife where true friendship was a permanent condition to be enjoyed forever.

I knew enough about mystical experiences to realize that it was happening to me. My heart expanded as Paul continued with his message. Everything came together. I already "knew"…somehow. And I realized that I had to know more and more.

I rushed up the riverbank toward the strong voice. I do have a way of swaying people off their feet, which is what I did to Paul and Luke. I mesmerized them when I told them how I was mesmerized by Paul. As I explained the details of my experience, there was no doubt that the gospel was in my heart. I and my household were baptized. My estate had many guest rooms, so I insisted that they stay with me. They readily agreed to remain with me as long as they could.

It was a lovely three months. Paul had time to relax in the mornings. He didn't have to make tents for his upkeep. Luke could paint. And they were free to teach and heal and organize the church all afternoon and evening. It was wonderful!

You all know the rest of the story. I am grateful for the prayers of the gospel people who interceded for the grace of my conversion. It is good here in heaven to develop a warm friendship with you all...and with Aristotle, too.

But only you, Good Father, know the loneliness— and sometimes the exaspera- tions—that dogged my steps. Yes, I did excel in everything I put my hand to. I was exceptional in my education and in my busi- ness. But it is difficult to be a leader, what with so much envy and backbiting. Other women among the Twenty-Eight have brought up the same problem. But my sadness was extra poignant. I was single, and I was relatively friendless. There was no husband to console me, to share my triumphs and heartaches...to just be there.

I had the same temptations that all gifted people seem to have. Because I was so orderly and quick to achieve, I had short pa- tience with the slovenly and the slow. Because I was a per- fectionist, I became over-disturbed by people who would settle for less. My lack of compassion seems to be the occupational haz- ard for all whose greatest comfort is their career. In turn, it sometimes spills over into self-doubts. I had many headaches, wondering what I was working so hard for. Who cares, anyway? If I die, what will happen to the business? Who will get my money? What will they live on? Why do I bother pushing, pushing, pushing people when they don't seem to be very concerned—so long as they get their paycheck?

Self-doubt and cynicism can be a strong temptation with career men and women who stay single. This cynicism can be the cause of many escapes from depression. Not knowing true compassion, they can become man-hunters or womanizers. They can let alcohol, overeating, or drugs be their consort after business hours. They are far more fragile than their cool, self-possessed demeanor shows. I know.

That is why they need your compassion, Good Father. Loneliness can be so harmful to a person. They need to know Jesus, as Paul proclaimed him to me. Their world of policies and products and the many concerns of staying successful can keep them preoccupied for too long.

Father, I can help them understand that you will be a comfort and a balance. If they accept our love, we will teach them about true friendship. They will then begin to enjoy life more as they wait for your kindness at their version of the bend in the river. I will help them experience the same things that changed my life. I know all the pitfalls of their careering. I know all the bends in the river, too.

Jesus Speaks

Ms. Careering, my dear Lydia, has said it well. Because of her background, she knows more, and loves deeper, than what she says. Let her be so commissioned, Father.

Now, I defer to my dear Paul. I can tell from his beaming smile that he has more to say.

Saint Paul Speaks

Indeed, my Lord. Lydia only hinted at the kindnesses she gave Luke and me. I want to publicly express my gratitude for the ways she endeared herself to us. Of course, compassion takes on many forms of expression. Hers was compassion of a most practical and efficient kind. Like herself. The best of her talents she put at our disposal. We were given a marvelous place to stay, where for ninety days we recuperated from many months of hardships, imprisonments, shipwrecks, and tortures.

There I had time to arrange my thoughts. Before going to Lydia's villa, I was preaching Christ and him crucified...day in and day out, without let-up. My preaching was spontaneous; words simply gushed forth from me, without much order. But in that relaxed atmosphere, I could reflect more deeply on what I had already said. I could appreciate new connections of what it means to live "in Christ." It was with Ms. Careering, and on her estate, that I evolved my outlines for the letters I would write later on.

Lydia was so kind, so encouraging. She was a good listener as well. She helped me with the "practical chapters" of my outlines. She knew people very well and the working situations of the Greek and Roman world. This was especially helpful. I was a product of strict Jewish training and knew my Scriptures, front to back. And, of course, I knew my own Jewish world. But I was naive about the world she knew so well.

Her compassion and encouragement helped Luke, also. Thanks to the luxury of those long sunlit hours every morning, he started illustrating scenes from the life of Christ, all those incidents surrounding the nativity, the parables, the exchanges with his disciples and the clashes with his enemies, the step-by-step details of the Passion—everything. It was from this initial doodling in the art-studio Lydia provided that he developed his orderly account of what we know to be Saint Luke's gospel. He never would have written it if it were not for our "resort of peace,"as we called Ms. Careering's home.

She is good, one of my favorite friends, and one of the very best when it comes to practical compassion.

God Speaks
So be it.

Lydia, be the instrument of my compassion for all those who devote their lives entirely to their carreers. And report periodically to the one I still call the Most Blessed among Women. I want Mary to keep her special care for the unmarried men and women who have decided to be so for the sake of the kingdom. John was the only apostle who remained single. And my son designated Mary to be his mother. In a special way, then, John stands for priests, nuns, sisters, and brothers who pledge themselves to celibacy so that they may concentrate more freely and fully on the church's ministries. They, too, must live out their careers as people of prayer, celebrators of my mysteries, channels of my mercy. They must regard their work above any other interest. They can be tempted to cynicism and self-doubt, no less than others, so we must bestow upon them our compassion, even as they are bringing it to others.

Mary will guide you, Lydia, in this most special branch of career individuals, whom I also consider my confidants, my servants, and my friends.

Agreed?

Mary, Lydia, and the saints in heaven respond with one voice, "Amen."

22 Not Dwelling on the Past

THE STORY OF

Ms. Once Was

THE WOMAN NOT CONDEMNED BY JESUS

The scribes and Pharisees brought a woman caught in adultery, and setting her in the middle of the crowd, said to Jesus, "Master, this woman was caught in adultery. In the law, Moses commanded us to stone such persons. What do you say?" [Jesus did not respond.] When they continued asking him, he...said to them, "Let him who is without sin among you be the first to cast a stone at her."...On hearing this, they went away, one by one.... Jesus, raising himself, said to her, "Woman, where are they? Has no one condemned you?" "No one, Lord," she said. Then Jesus said, "Neither do I condemn you. Go your way; and from now on, sin no more."   John 8: 1-11

Ms. Once Was Speaks
Good Father, for this new commission, call me "Ms. Once Was." Just for fun. The element of fun—that element of fun by which we can laugh at ourselves—is what is needed most among the people I shall serve.

My case, of course, has been well known since John's gospel was written, at least the turning point of my case is celebrated. There was quite a controversy about me for centuries. Many so-called staunch defenders of morality did not want Christ's mercy

---

linked so closely with a repugnant sinner like myself. They worried about the scandal it might give; perhaps it would encourage more adultery and thus break up other homes.

But the Holy Spirit, inspiring wiser, kinder minds, made sure that Christ's compassion had its say. I stayed in the gospel.

But people understand me only at the big moment of my turn-about. They see me at the day I hit bottom, so to speak, facing the prospect of ritual execution for my sins. Then the readers rejoice with me as Jesus raised me up from my state of dereliction and put me on the path to full recovery. My story is similar to alcoholics, drug addicts, compulsive eaters, gamblers, shoppers...self-abusers of all sorts. I hit bottom in my particular compulsion. Then I was connected to a real experience with my "higher power"; Jesus forgave me. He did not condemn me the way others did—or the way I condemned myself.

I was released from my degenerate lifestyle and given the hope to live without the burden of my bad instincts. And I grew, little by little, in self-mastery. I also developed an honest analysis of my past, and began to want to help others who still suffer in the way I once did.

I accomplished a lot of good during those years after my conversion. But at times, I was a terrible bore as well. It was so tempting for me to rehash the story of my conversion—over and over—to any group or any individual who were targets for my earnestness. For a while (a long while) I became a snob. I felt superior to people whose sins were not as spectacular as mine. I looked down my nose at their lacklustre peccadillos. They could not understand the depths of my degradation. "Poor things," I thought,

"They can't really appreciate what they have, because they never lost it the way I did!"

I was quick to bend the ears of those who were going down the same path of compulsion that used to master me. Riding over their feelings, I would aggressively roll out my story and try to pulverize their defenses with the logic of my steps of self-improvement.

Then, as you well know, Father, Jesus met me after Easter. That would have been a little over a year after my change in lifestyle. He praised me for avoiding my sin. He added to his original warnings, though; he wanted me to stop telling everybody how I was avoiding sin.

He begged me to lighten up—to have more fun—to blend a sense of humor and a large dose of compassion into my seriousness. I saw his point. That Easter visit marked the second stage of my conversion: I enrolled, at last, in the mainstream of humanity. I no longer consider myself special because of the dramatic circumstances of my past. I learned to be kind to everyone. It took a lot of patience to empathize with those whose lives were far more drab and less adventurous than mine. But I did it, and grew because of it.

Compassion is a most beautiful virtue, Father. But it is complicated. I can see why you need so many volunteers for your new commission. Mercy is exercised in such different ways.

Some of my Care People I have already hinted at. I want to be with all the celebrated sinners of the world: all addicts who have hit bottom and then come back to a reasonably well-adjusted life. I'll be with them mostly as an encourager. These people are the best qualified to care for others who are wrestling with the problems they were so familiar with. I want to praise them for the good they do in their support groups; I want to bless them for their sacrifice of energy and time as they continue to counsel the individuals under their care. I want to help them carry on, despite the ups and downs (and sometimes even their failures) they will have.

But I also want to help them have compassion for others who are *not* like them. They need to learn longsuffering for the rest of the world's woes, too. They need to balance their "specialness" and put aside the thought of "What I once was" so that they can enjoy the ordinary ways that people joke with one another and keep traditions and regulate the time machines of their work and pleasures. This kind of compassion takes patience, kindness toward all, and the forgiveness of sins, which are different from their own.

I also want to reach out to another category of "once was" personalities: those who in middle age sigh regretfully for the lost joys when they were beauty queens or star athletes or in other ways had their brief moments of distinction in their youth. The bright light of former years has faded, so they prefer to replay their past than to really live in the (sometimes) dull circumstancess of their present time.

They need compassion—*straight*—my God, large draughts of it! Individuals who boast, "I once was a great sinner, or a notorious compulsive... and now I've changed"—these people can be dull company. They are predictable because they are repetitive. But there is hope in them, and optimism; they revel in the present time of their new life.

But those who replay their tapes of "I was once a great football star, or dancer, or life of the party, or big spender, or whatever... and now I'm a nobody!"...well, these individuals are dreary as well as dull. The present time exists for them mostly as occasions for regret, in contrast to their more lively bygone days.

They need to know our compassion, Father, and quickly, for the time is short. There is so much good that they can do if only they restrain that debilitating nostalgia. I'll try to show them that we love them—for the good they can do now, as well as for the "stars" they used to be. Our love does not depend on spectacular performance or enthusiastic moods. They need to be encouraged to live in their more modest means and less exhilarating possibilities. Some people need compassion to be more patient with others; these people need it to be more patient with themselves.

For both categories of "I once was a great sinner" and "I once was a great star," we will reset their time machines so that they will not focus so firmly on their past, but will see their world as a time to be lived in—in the present.

Let me begin, Good Father. The past has gone. The task is now. The time is short.

Jesus Speaks

Yes, Father, let Once Was be so commissioned. I will have to ask her to tone down, somewhat, her own sense of fun. People who resent the present because they so strongly relive the past—these people don't have much of a sense of humor. Also, judgmental people find it most difficult to laugh at themselves and to take the world as it is given to them. They don't have time to look at themselves, because they always want to change the world. So my friend must be very patient with their impatience.

There is so much goodness in these converted sinners and addicts. All we need to do is to help them with perspectives.

God Speaks

Begin, Ms. Once Was. Do all you can to bring your people into balance and patience with their present possibilities.

I ask for all assembled to pray for those "once was" people who cannot be reached in any other way than prayer. I speak now of the sinners who are still in their sins…and don't even want my Son's pardon and peace. I speak of alcoholics and other addicts who are intent on ruining their lives—who don't want to change, don't even wish they could. I speak of the aged who are so bitter about their actual poverty or maladies or the injustices done to them that they cannot find any relief by thinking about any part of their past. That's their problem. We can neither heal their memories or give them hope for the future. All time is bleak for them.

Citizens of heaven, pray for them and do what you can to get your friends on earth to pray also. We cannot interfere with free will. We want to give them our compassion, but we won't force it on them. We only hope and pray that they will change.

One other thing: find ways and means to reach those people (like the families of alcoholics) who face the harmful consequences of addictive personalities. Show them we have compassion for them, too. We understand their sorrows and frustrations, and sometimes their financial doom. We will help them all we can. It may not happen overnight. It may not happen until they get to heaven. But let them know, for certain, that some day they will never suffer: never, any more.

Let all of us be so assigned. There is much to do. There are many to pray for.

The citizens of heaven say: "Amen."

THE STORY OF

The Searcher

PILATE'S WIFE

Pilate knew that the scribes and Pharisees had delivered up Jesus because of envy. Now, as he was sitting on the judgment seat, his wife went to him, saying, "Have nothing to do with that just man, for I have suffered many things in a dream because of him."   Matthew 27:18-19

The Searcher Speaks
Good Father, compared to most members of this commission, my Care Persons will be a smallish group, but important, just the same. Prayer is important; matters of the Spirit are important; so they are important.

I was a searcher for spiritual growth ever since I can remember. My household gods and goddesses were most dear to me. I was born a Roman (as I used to say) by the favor of Caesar and the grace of Juno. I hated the fights in the arena. I was nauseated by the victory parades of captives and monkeys and elephants. But the simple pieties at home and the quiet appeals of the Vestal Virgins moved me deeply when I was a child. I knew that God was present, somehow, in all the mishmash of the many dieties competing for attention.

But this was not enough. In my late twenties, I married Pontius Pilate. Not long afterward, he was ordered to the trouble spot in the Middle East. He hated the prospect; the zealots among the Jews and Herod's unpredictability made it a despised assignment. My outlook was quite different. I was excited about the journey east. The religion of the Jews fascinated me. They were so confident in their certitude. They worshipped one God, only one. No chance for competition or jealousies. I liked that. But even though their faith was simple, their codes of behavior were too complex, too exacting. I was curious to discover how their religion was practiced in their chief city.

Also, there were many other fascinating religions and styles of prayer in that part of the world. Mystics of all kinds thrived. When I arrived, I learned that a short carriage ride would give me access to fortune-tellers, dream interpreters, followers of Persian-style Buddhism, sun worshippers, astrologers who claimed control over the universe, specialists in breathing exercises, ministers of the occult—even functionaries of a strange, erotic religion that combined the body cult of the Greeks with the preoccupation for health foods and diets, which is the corruption of the Jewish kosher system.

I tried them all. I was helped most by the religions that taught me how to quiet down and pray. These meditations helped me greatly. My group would take a text in praise of God and say it over and over and then let inspiration come. I was very faithful to these centering exercises. Sometimes—it was just a feeling—I drew closer to a sense of God and of God's goodness in creation. Sometimes there seemed to be a message meant for me.

Such messages came in the form of dreams. Sometimes they were actual dreams, when I was waking up. Sometimes it was more like a fantasy when I was awake, but it seemed like a dream. I didn't know what to do about these puzzling presentiments. I had no counsellor, no spiritual director to guide me.

Oh, many individuals volunteered to interpret the messages, but they were contradictory in what they said. Anyway, I did not trust them. I longed for someone who would be wise and kind, gentle and challenging. Nobody! My husband was worse than useless. He didn't believe in any God; he didn't even believe in himself. All he did was mock my seriousness.

He did this very thing when he returned home on what we now call Good Friday afternoon. I had a dream the evening before—at the very time when Jesus gave his flesh to eat and spoke about his love to the apostles. I dreamed: "A just man was going to be crucified." That's all I knew. The message didn't tell me what to do, only that someone would soon be killed and that he did not deserve to die.

I had no direction at the time, so I just assumed I was supposed to prevent some injustice from taking place. The next morning, I learned that Jesus of Nazareth was on trial. This had to be the Just Man in my dreams. I sent my husband the message, choosing the most persuasive servant to deliver my note. Pilate read it and listened carefully to what my messenger said. He was moved...but he was weak. The threats of the Pharisees and the anger of the crowd was too compelling. He caved in to pressure. (As usual.)

Then he came home and tried to justify his conduct—to himself more than to me. He ridiculed my "superstitious behavior." I had nothing to fall back on but my own certitude that my message came from God. It seemed that I was supposed to wash my hands of the whole incident, but I could not get it out of my mind.

Then I heard rumors that the Just Man had risen from the dead. My husband laughed at this. He reminded me of all the other gods and goddesses who claimed the same distinction. He said this was just a Jewish version of the same old hope for life after death. He dismissed it. He then ordered his troops to stamp out any popular uprising that might occur.

I couldn't dismiss it. I searched for someone to tell me more about this resurrected Just Man. Then I met Nathaniel—one of the apostles, the one they call "guileless"—coming from the market. Something drew me to him. His eyes told me that he had those qualities—wise and kind, gentle and challenging—that I had been seeking.

I asked him outright, "Please, sir, tell me about the man in my dreams." He was indeed without guile. Even though he took a great risk talking to a Roman stranger, Nathaniel told me all I needed to know. And he did so as though he were familiar with my heart. He seemed to know all my experiences of searching for a God I only vaguely understood.

He explained the name "Just Man" by referring to Isaiah and the other prophets. One man would take on all the sins of all the world and die a cruel death in order to restore a bridge of trust between God and humankind. By the crucifixion of this one man, life beyond death was promised to everyone. As Nathaniel unrolled his story of what happened—all that Jesus said to his disciples after the resurrection—I knew that the vague hopes in my heart were coming true, at last. Nathaniel agreed to be my spiritual director.

I met Peter and the others, and even talked with Paul. I grew in grace from the experience. The small community was good to me and accepted me. Then the apostles disbanded for fear of persecution. I wanted to leave my husband and join them in their travels, but they said no. "Stay with Pilate," they said. "He will soon be ordered to return to Rome. We may need you there." So I stayed with Pilate, and as it turned out, they did need me in Rome. I used my influence when, first Peter, then Paul, arrived. I could not get them out of prison, but they had comfortable quarters and could receive visitors, without restrictions.

My husband had died before any of these last events. I was free to practice my faith openly...and to be a person of influence for my friends. Then came Nero and his paranoid atrocities. And I was martyred. Because I was of a noble Roman family, I was not degraded; they did not feed me to the beasts. Privately, they simply cut off my head.

And now that I am here in heaven, I see how all my journeys and searching, everything about the push and pull of my life, now makes sense. My story is unique, as all stories of spiritual maturity are. But there is enough about my story that is common to all searchers. I know their self-doubts. I know their tendency to be quickly dissatisfied with the lack of progress and with the dark nights of alienation that afflict them at times. I know their need for a spiritual director as good as Nathaniel...and how seldom they are able to find one.

It is a hard journey that searchers for growth must travel. I know. So, Good Father, I want to give them your compassion, and mine, too. I cannot give them spiritual consolation all the time.

You won't permit that, Father; it would not be good for them. If they were always consoled, they would gravitate toward relishing their consolation for its own sake, instead of continuing in search of a purer love for you.

The consolation they need is the kind Nathaniel gave me: true understanding of the Suffering Servant. They will learn how patient endurance and intrepid loyalty to prayer are the mainstays of their spiritual progress. I will help them in whatever way I can to experience the truth that becoming close to you, my Lord, will more than make up for the pain of remaining constant. You will be with them and bless them in their search.

Jesus Speaks

Yes, Good Father, let Searcher be selected for these most gifted people who want to grow in prayer. And let us together—you and I and the Holy Spirit—make special efforts to induce young people to choose this path. It is never easy. There are no quick results, no instant satisfactions. But so many young people have high ideals and are willing to make sacrifices—to "pump iron" in order to earn an athletic scholarship, to diet fiercely for the chance to be a beauty queen. Let them discipline themselves even harder for a goal that is much, much higher.

When they achieve competence in prayerfulness, we can be confident about an ever-fresh company of contemplatives. This way, we will have more people to talk to, more joy to share.

God Speaks

Yes. As you say, Son. And as you wish, my charming Searcher of good dreams, I only add that special consideration be given to those who have become drop-outs in their search. They were fervent for a while, and they did reach altitudes—sometimes high altitudes—of mystical intimacy. Then dryness dragged them away from their resolutions. Or other attitudes intruded, other pressures and pursuits (even noble ones) that impeded their time for prayer. We must find a way to reach them also, and return them to divine reflectiveness that they used to search for...and then stopped trying to attain.

Citizens of heaven, let us be united in this noble pursuit of uniting all people to this divine reflectiveness.

And the angels and saints respond, "Amen."

24　Feeling Lonely

THE STORY OF

Mrs. Left Back

SAINT ANDREW'S WIFE

Looking upon Jesus as he walked by, [John the Baptist] said, "Behold the Lamb of God." And the two disciples followed Jesus. Jesus...seeing them, said to them, "What is it you seek?" They said to him, "Master, where do you dwell?" He  said to them, "Come and see." And they stayed with him that day. It was about four in the afternoon. [The next day] Andrew, the brother of Simon Peter, who was one of the two...went to his brother Simon and said, "We have found the Messiah."
John 1: 35-41

Mrs. Left Back Speaks
Father, my Lord, wars are going on in the world, as you know; always wars are going on. So there are always families who worry as their loved ones take part in battle. There are others who must leave home for reasons other than war. This leaves the stay-at-homes

---

who have the drudgery of normal routine and the burdens of added domestic responsibilities. I am also concerned about parents when their children grow up, get married, and start their own families. In all of these cases, the ones who are left behind must readjust to a difficult, sometimes worrisome, always a changed world. These are the people I want to help, Good Father.

Everyone in heaven knows me as Leah, wife of Andrew the apostle. But for this work, let me be called "Mrs. Left Back." I can't be called "Left Out," since I have never felt estranged from Andrew. But I stayed home while my husband followed Jesus up and down the countryside. Our children understood. They made me proud, taking their father's place and becoming seasoned fishermen almost overnight. Our parents understood, too. Indeed, all the families of the apostles went along with our abrupt change in our lives. It was something our men had to do. We couldn't keep them home, even if we wanted to. Jesus called them to follow him. We knew, instinctively—before he had worked any of his signs—that he was the chosen one of God. I could never go against that!

Just the same, it was hard to say goodbye. I loved Andrew so much. I loved the normal, ordinary things we did...as day followed day, season replaced season, feast days were prepared for, and simple joys were shared.

Now all this was gone, never to be the same. Oh, Andrew did come home every now and then and fill us in on the news. The Lord was not so demanding of their time that he didn't give them a three-day furlough at times. They would break their routine, especially after one of their more arduous journeys: through the inhospitable country of the Samaritans, or in the cities of Judea where the clever Scribes kept trying to trip them up. Anyway, Andrew would come home and it was always a joy to have him back; but it was different. We were different, too.

I was proud of my husband. I was worried also. Gossip arrived at our doorstep every day, much of it garbled. This added to my fears. As the last year approached, the leaders of our people were filled with more and more hatred against our cause. There were strong rumors that Jesus and his disciples were marked for death.

We had to manage, somehow, without my man to help me. He was the best at knowing how to do things. Jesus relied on his abilities, just as I did. He was the one in charge whenever Jesus took Peter, James, and John off by themselves. He was the expert in logistics—the overseer, you might say. And, until Joanna and the other women came to help out, he was in charge of the groceries and the cooking, too.

Meanwhile, I didn't have these services. All my years of married life, I depended on him for so much. Now I had to learn on my own. It wasn't easy. I just plodded along...and had a list of questions to ask when he came home again.

After Easter, I joined Andrew, with all my family, except for the two oldest, who kept the business going. We were all a part of the Pentecost experience. I could feel, firsthand, the great gifts that God was giving the world. I spoke in tongues. I worked signs of wonders, too.

It was wonderful to live out the rest of my life this way. New energy came to me. Andrew and I served others as we never did before; we had a sense of urgency to do God's will. We felt a joy that nothing could take from us. And when we died—together—we didn't doubt that Jesus would make good his promise of everlasting life. And, of course, he did...for here we are.

My story, Father, is a simple one. I speak for all who are "left back" home. Without question, every story of the "waiting ones" is unique and quite complex in its particulars. How their loved ones left them and what the demands of their new challenges would be are different in every case. No two people have the same physical or emotional particulars. Even so, they all need one kind of tenderness from us, Good Father: our compassion for that "left back home" grief which is as much a part of their lives as breathing...and sighing.

Let us reach them with fresh awareness that they are in good company. They are not alone, since many others the world over suffer from the same loneliness, the same worrisome concerns. It will be good for them to share their stories, if not their dreams, with people who suffer the same way.

And they will never be away from us, Good Father. I will go to them; and you are with them, even as I speak, continuing to inspire them, especially after they have been forced to adjust to the new demands life puts on them. And when their loved ones come back home to them, you will be with them at that crossroad, too. They may want to return to the good old days, to keep things just as they used to be, but this can never happen. They will have to prepare themselves for a new lifestyle and adapt, just as Andrew and I had to after Easter.

We will be with them, all the way, consoling them in every adjustment they must make. And when they die—together or apart—your blessed son will bring them here to be with us, where every panic will give way to peace, where wars can't happen, where there are no leave-takings whatsoever, and where nothing can ever take away their joy!

Jesus Speaks

Yes, Father, let Andrew and his wife continue in the wonderful ministry they had ever since Pentecost began to change the world. Indeed, even before this. When I gave my men their R. & R., I would go back to Nazareth to be with my mother, to get some rest and sleep in my own bed, to catch up on things at home. Then, on the afternoon before we all journeyed off again, I always went to Andrew's house to stay overnight with them. Leah was a very charming hostess; I felt easy in her company.

I am certain that all the people who are "left back home"—because of wars, or business concerns, or because their children grow up and move out, for whatever reason they are left alone—will be comforted by Leah. She will go into the kitchen, put on the tea kettle, cozy into slippers, and cheer them up with some good, practical kitchen-table conversations.

God Speaks

Thank you, my beloved Son. You make it sound so appealing. Perhaps we can gather in her kitchen after this meeting is over.

One item to add. St. Andrew, I want you to gather a subcommittee to serve another group of "left back home" people: those who are irrevocably severed. The people your wife will care for are those who expect their loved ones to return at some time. They may, or may not: soldiers are killed, accidents happen, offspring may never, or seldom, come home; but there is always hope.

Other individuals, though, cannot feed their prayers with this expectation. They are the ones whose loved ones died. They are also the jilted people, those who suffer from a severed relationship, which is almost the same thing as death. A marriage ends in divorce. An engagement is broken. A priest leaves the priesthood, a nun her order. A cherished friendship has been so badly damaged it cannot be restored. Whenever these separations occur, there is no hope for a reunion. Those involved in them must gather their lives as best they can and go on.

Such people can experience great sadness, especially in the beginning of their new lives. Their routine is disrupted beyond recall. Memories of many traditions—even the ways they used to share their suppertimes—now seem to mock them and make their loneliness even more poignant.

They need our compassion, most of all. See to it, Andrew, that they do not feel so rejected. Get them to pray more. Inspire them with hope. Help them to feel a self-reliance, a flexible creativity, and a courage they never knew they had. We will be with them. Help them to trust us—and themselves—a little better.

The citizens of heaven respond, "Amen."

25 When You're Criticized
No Matter What You Do

Ms. Shouldda

THE WOMAN WHO ANOINTED JESUS

As Jesus sat at table, a woman came with an alabaster jar of ointment of pure nard, very costly. She broke the jar and poured it over his head. But when the disciples saw this, they were indignant. They said, "Why this waste? This ointment might have been sold for more than 300 denarii (equal to the annual salary of the average worker) and given to the poor!" And they reproached her. But Jesus said, "Let her alone and do not trouble her. She has done a beautiful thing to me....She has anointed my body for burial....Wherever the gospel is preached, what she has done will be told in memory of her."   Matthew 26:6ff; Mark 14:3ff; John 12:1ff

Ms. Shouldda Speaks
Good Father, I am so glad you decided to establish this commission. At last, Jesus' words about me will come true. He wanted my good deed to have a lasting impact; he hoped that my generosity would always be appreciated.

It wasn't then. And it hasn't been for all these centuries. It seems that everybody in the whole world just flips right by with hardly a glance at the love I gave our Lord. He specifically remarked that I was supposed to be remembered...and I am still pretty much ignored.

I was even more insulted on the night itself. The apostles and I are great friends, now, but it wasn't always so. Something happens to people—even to good people like the apostles—whenever there is news of a generous donation to a noble cause. Whenever this takes place, it seems to bring out the mean-hearted shrewdness in us...a kind of comparative shopping critique.

The gospel called my jar of ointment of pure nard a costly gift. It was! The men who watched me spill the contents on Jesus' head and neck immediately started working figures in their minds. Quick estimates rounded out a notable sum: over 300 denarii, the annual salary of an average worker. In modern currency, this would come to about 12 to 14 thousand dollars.

I was glad to anoint Jesus like this. I could afford it and I *wanted* to do it. Jesus said I was preparing his body for an honorable burial, after his most dishonorable execution.

Well, that's how it turned out. But I was doing it for the day ahead, not for the burial. I watched Jesus closely over the week that went before. He was exhausted: teaching the people all day, answering loaded questions from his violent antagonists, praying in Gethsemane most of the night. Such a schedule took its toll; there were bags under his eyes, slumping shoulders. It was an effort for him just to put one leg in front of the other as he walked up the hill of Cedron.

I knew he had planned to have a special night with his disciples; the meal would be most important. He shared with me some of his thoughts about love that he was going to bring up.

I wanted to ease his tension, to relax his muscles, his tense jaw and tired shoulders. I was really preparing him for his Passover Meal, not for his death.

It worked. The gentle rubdown invigorated him and he thanked me. That was reward enough. But nobody else thanked me or praised me. The disciples scolded me. Oh, they meant well. Everybody means well when they second-guess somebody who has contributed to a noble cause. Instinctively everybody always showers recriminations on the benefactor—they say. "You should have done this or that with the money you spent on the ointment!" In my case, the apostles scolded me because I should have fed the poor instead of wasting it with a one-time massaging that relieved their Lord and Master's tensions.

So I ask you, Father, call me "Ms. Shouldda" for this commission. Wealthy people have great need for our compassion. Their money is not unlimited. They have to select certain causes or endow particular persons to benefit from their charity. No sooner do these wealthy contributors pick their one or two charities, when a thousand other causes resent being robbed of their rights. "The money *shouldda* been given to us!" they argue (often vehemently). "Our needs are far more important than anybody else's!"

If money is donated to the church, it should have been spent on the poor. If it is given to the poor, it should have gone to research. If money is donated to foreign missions, there are suffering people at home who are forced to starve because of such misplaced benefactions. Or vice versa. Nobody is immune from second-guessers. Spend ten dollars for one cause, and a hundred voices cry "foul!" because the money didn't go to them.

My concern, Good Father, is not only for the rich who are treated so contemptibly after they have done good deeds. I will care for all people, of whatever financial bracket, who are shamefully scolded after their expenditure of energy. It is not only money that brings out people's jealousy. Time is valuable, too. If a husband spends time helping youngsters in the inner city playground, people will say he should have spent the time with his family. If a wife agrees to chair a campaign for the needs of a hospital, husband and children gripe about being left out.

On the other hand, if the spouses stay at home, sharing quality time with their family, they will be criticized for not doing more for noble causes outside their comfortable, safe homes. There is no lack of voices claiming priority for volunteers. These people can sometimes make the sturdiest of souls feel guilty.

Grandparents complain that their families should spend more time with them, and less with the other grandparents. Children can get into a fierce rivalry because Mom "takes better care of my baby sister (or my handicapped brother) than she does of me!" It could go on and on.

Understood this way—in terms of contributing time and energy as well as money—nobody is excluded. Everyone suffers from the "sadness of the Shoulddas."

Let me be a balm for them, Good Father. I cannot give them $14,000 worth of precious ointment. I live in the Spirit-world now. But I can do for them what Jesus did for me that evening so long ago. While everybody else chided me for my generosity, he—*only* he—thanked me. His blessing was enough. I was content, even before he ordered the rest of the room to change their attitude about what I did...even before he commanded that the whole world praise me for my lavish gift.

I want all people to understand my Lord's most gracious ways. This is the compassion they need. Just to realize that Jesus knows all about their kindness and the desire to help people with their time and energy. Once they experience Christ's blessing on their deeds and good intentions, they won't get so demoralized by other people's snipes of jealousy.

I will help them settle for the best of blessings. And I will see them through each expenditure—given for the sake of love. If they still feel bad because of criticism, I will help them wait for the only time and place when they will get universal approval for the good they do. The time is out-of-time. The place is here, with us...for all eternity.

Jesus Speaks
Well said, my dear, dear friend. I hope all people get to hear your speech. I have tried, very hard, to have your name and what you did much better known. I have pushed your cause. I made sure that the evangelists did not neglect to mention your kindness to me. Only a little imaginative prayer is needed to understand what that soothing lotion meant to me. It put energy back into my tired frame. I was recharged with a sense of my dignity and the nobility of my purpose.

My passion and death, which followed soon after, gave me a sense of frustration and degradation. I couldn't get my apostles to listen to my words; they were too depressed to really hear me. I then agonized in the Garden of Gethsemane, knowing what cruel taunts and bitter hatreds would send me to my death. I felt so abandoned on the cross, where my instincts told me to cry out to my Father to change his gentle plan of love and turn me into a powerful vindicator who would come down from the cross and express how I feel about sin.

And then I thought of the last time I was honored. It was your gift of precious nard, my dear one. That is what drew my heart and head to prevail over my instincts. And in that wretched thirst, choking up my last breath, I died with composure, remaining constant to my Father's plan of love.

I know I comforted you when I came to your defense that night. Now I want you to help others feel good about themselves. Donating good things to others is a tricky business; it can often be misunderstood. Even my own apostles misunderstood what you were doing. This must be changed, or else the whole spirit of generosity will dry up. Let us work together, my beloved lavisher of nard, to make it easier for people to do good works and feel our gratitude for their courtesy and generosity.

God Speaks

So be it, Ms. Shouldda. I am delighted that my Son wants to cooperate so closely. He is always for the down-trodden, the poor and marginalized. It is important that the world know that God is also for people of means, the benefactors, the doers of good in all areas of life.

One more group has not been discussed, among the many categories of those who "shouldda." These people claim my own special attention. These are the ones—practically everybody—who browbeat themselves with personal recriminations. So many, many people don't need critics to chide them, or second-guessers to contradict their decisions in life; they do it to themselves. Some giveaway statements go like this: "I 'shouldda' been kinder to my children....I 'shouldda' married somebody else....I 'shouldda' taken that job when it was offered....I 'shouldda' refused that first drink....I 'shouldda' been braver, stronger, more disciplined early on, less busy with my work, more helpful to my family." On and on the chorus of regrets rises from their world of wishes. This saddens me.

Please, Shouldda, enlist more volunteers to help you convince these people that a thousand sighs and ten thousand "shoulddas" cannot bring back one yesterday. I want them to relax, confess their sins, learn from their past as best they can...and get on with the job of living in their own real world. We do have compassion to give them, and forgiveness of sins. Let them forgive themselves and then go on, no longer slaves of their own wishful thinking.

The citizens of heaven sing out fervently, "Amen."

THE STORY OF

Widow Little

THE WIDOW WHO GAVE HER LITTLE BIT

Jesus glanced up and saw the rich putting their offering into
the treasury, and also a poor widow putting in two copper
coins. At that he said, "I assure you, this poor widow has
put in more than all the rest. For they have given out of their
abundance, but she, out of her want, has given all that she
had—all that she had to live on."

Mark 12:41-44; Luke 21:1-4

The Widow Little Speaks
Good Father, permit me to enter my name to this list of gospel
women who will find new approaches for manifesting your compassion. I feel so insignificant in the presence of the others, but
that's the way I always was. And, probably because of this, there
are people I can reach better than anyone, since I have lived their
ways so closely.

I never even met the Lord; I was just somebody in the crowd—
somebody Jesus happened to notice one day. I was out of earshot
before I had a chance to hear him praise me. His comment was
that I was "The Widow Little," even on this occasion. The "widow's mite" is associated with me. Yes, two copper pennies were
all I had to give. I was not poor to the point of begging. I had
enough clay, back home, to make more cups and dishes to sell on

the streets. But those coins were all that I had in cash; that was what I gave for upkeep of God's holy temple. It was not a big deal, not even a modest sacrifice. I was just doing my duty. That's what I always did.

Jesus used the occasion for his own purposes, which had little to do with me. He was telling the proud Pharisees, who always put their good deeds on display, that God's way of judging motives and behavior is much different from the world's. He also demonstrated, for the benefit of his disciples, that he knew everything about everybody—even the insides of their pocketbooks and souls.

All well and good. But I want to be known as somebody more than just a little old woman who was generous one day! I want to enlarge my role as the Widow Little for all the little people in the world. Good Father, you did say, in your opening words, that there would be some interweaving of responsibilities. That's true. My friend Justa and I will have close ties. But with a difference. She will concentrate on the whole range of people who downplay themselves as "just a housewife," "just a worker," "just a teenager."

My Care People will be mostly older people: widows and widowers, for the most part, and all the unattached, the sickly-old, those who settle down to a fixed routine...and let life ebb away on them. When they are asked, "How are you?" they answer, "Okay, I guess. Nothing much going on." When they go to confession, they prefix their remarks with, "I don't have many sins; I don't do much any more." They have their own set schedule. Nothing much excites them. That's how they characterize themselves: "nothing much." Loneliness is a way of life for them, a desert of boredom with occasional oases of family visits, an early supper out, phone calls from old friends, check-ups with their doctor. Nothing much.

Father, they do not need a strong shot of your compassion. They shouldn't be shaken too strongly out of their modest lethargy, or challenged into some new change of life; their hearts couldn't take the shock. A regular routine is the crutch that helps them manage. They can no more change their ways than I could change my routine of getting up to pray in the early morning, performing my accustomed acts of worship, working three hours on my clay and then going to market to sell my wares, chatting with my few friends in the stalls beside me, then coming home to eat alone at the end of the day. (It was so hard to eat, because I felt so miserable then—missing my husband and the children, seeing my life so barren and unattractive...so alone.)

I speak for those who live as I used to live. They don't need a jolt of new life, Father; they need tender  hints of your compassion; they need to know more about your Son and his love; they need to know him the way I learned about him, soon after I heard about his praise for my generosity. Jesus notices the little things we do. He cares about us in those activities we categorize as "just going through the motions." He can inoculate the aging against despair.

That is the big danger for my people: the fear that soon their little world will change from "nothing much" into "nothing at all." They keep memorizing their past, with all its long-ago liveliness, because that is where the action was. And now, as life is receding, their hopes shrivel up as well.

Only when they hear your Son's statement about true finalities will they find their dignity again. Routine will some day change into crippling old age, which will end in death. But death will not be the end of everything. They will learn from us, Father, that new life awaits them, thanks to the saving power of Jesus. They will experience a return to the best of what their lives once were...and, added to that, they will be endowed with a capacity for joy and beauty that cannot even be imagined in their present circumstances.

If they allow it, Father, I will nudge the awareness of eternity into the pattern of their fixed routine. Our compassion will take two forms: I will assure them of Jesus' appreciation for the little things they do, all the ways they notice others and help them. This will console them, knowing that we appreciate them. Also, I will nourish them with new prospects for their future—the long, long future here in heaven. Their life does not end in death, but with Jesus praising them for much more than their patient endurance and their sacrifices. Jesus will praise them for who they *are*, as he helps them to appreciate their own loveliness.

And he will welcome them, as he did me, to the place where loneliness is no longer...where littleness is made much of...where boredom is impossible...and where all their tears, grieving for what we missed, will be washed away and reshaped into joy.

Jesus Speaks

Yes, Father, this is good. The Widow Little is a fine example of your wisdom in forming this new committee. I never suffered from the dull throb of boredom in old age. I was never a widower who missed his wife and found it difficult to eat at home once the kitchen became a mockery of past life. I died young with no personal experience of what the Widow Little went through during the last third of her long life. She knows all these things firsthand. Let her have every grace she needs, every means at our disposal, to put the hope of heaven into the "nothing much to live for any more" mood that saddens so many people—young and old—so much of the time.

The widowed and the alienated are most precious to our hearts. Let our compassion visit them and stay with them in friendship. They have more work to do on earth, more love to give. I have already blessed the world of their routine. Our grace will let them fill out the rest of their lives more gently.

God Speaks

Yes. So be it. As usual, my Son, you have said exactly what I meant to say. Begin, Widow Little. There are millions who will need your tenderness. I will give you all the help you need.

One more thing. Set a special group aside to comfort the senior citizens who mourn for other reasons than for the joys that used to be. I speak of single people who regret not having married, and some married people whose memories are crowded with bitterness about the way their lives went sour. It is hard enough to live alone, when happiness-that-was is just a memento taunting their present life. It is much more difficult to face the boredom of old age with no good memories to fall back on.

They need our promise of happy ending more than anyone. Enlist the saints who come from a history of battered childhood, broken homes, brutal or impossible-to-live-with spouses. That is, ask all our citizens of heaven who know what it means to live out the last years with nothing but miserable memories of what went before. We want our compassion to be their pillow during this time of their lives, and we want Christ's power of resurrection to be their deathbed. Amen."

The citizens of heaven agree: "Amen."

THE STORY OF

Ambition

THE MOTHER OF JAMES AND JOHN

The mother of James and John came to Jesus with her sons and, worshipping, she made a request of him: "Command that these, my two sons, may sit, one at your right hand and one at your left hand, in your kingdom." Jesus answered, "You do not know what you are asking for. Can you drink of the cup that I am about to drink?" They said to him, "We can." He said to them, "You shall...." Matthew 20:20-28

Ambition Speaks
Good Father, let me be simply called "Ambition" as an agent of your compassion. Not "Ms." or "Mrs." or anything indicating sex; ambition is not the prerogative of either sex. To have ambition is not all bad. It is one of the muscles of idealism, the power impelling all great works. To have ambition is not all good, either. It is linked with the desire for control, it can easily obliterate the more sensitive virtues, such as love, a desire to serve others, a sense of humor...and patient endurance in this less than perfect world.

I was ambitious once. For a long time, I lived with the good and the bad sides of it. My sons were strong and hardy, impetuous, too—prone to flares of temper. Even Jesus nicknamed them "sons of thunder." But I could handle them; I was the "thunder" they were the sons of.

They took to sea, a natural thing for them to do. Our village had only one prominent industry: fishing. I made sure they were the best in the business. It was a good life, for some years. We had one of the nicest homes in town. People deferred to me in the marketplace. They paid attention to my comments about politics and finance. That was about as much as I could hope to accomplish: to be a good wife, a reliable neighbor, a gracious hostess on all occasions, and a mother who brought up children anyone would be proud of. I was friendly, efficient, astute, and acted kindly to everyone (as long as they did not cross me).

Then Jesus came along and took my sons away from me. Just like that! I was upset by this. Indeed, I was angry. But the mood lasted only for a half an afternoon. My faith in God and my trust in God's promises were too real for me to block out anything the Lord might want from me. It was plain to see that Jesus was very special. Maybe—or maybe not—he was the Messiah we had all prayed for.

If he turned out to be a hoax, we'd know it soon enough. I would keep the business with Zebedee, and my sons would return in due time. But if Jesus was truly what James and John said he was, I did not dare to interfere.

I joined the going-away party held in Andrew's house. I was the one who told Jesus that Peter's mother-in-law was sick in bed. There were two reasons for asking Jesus to heal my friend. I wanted her to join in the festivities; she would have been so hurt if she were left out. I also wanted to check out Jesus' credentials, you might say. I knew Sacred Scripture very well. I watched Jesus closely to see if he would work a miracle...and to see how he would do it.

When I observed his gentleness and his absolute command over a fever, I was convinced. No acrobatic piety, no big commotion, no trickery. Just a simple word, a kind smile, a helping hand. Only the effortless re-creative touch of God.

After this, I became a champion of the cause. If my sons nursed any second thoughts about following Jesus, I would have packed their duffle bags for them. It didn't take me long to conjure up what possibilities would lie ahead. There would soon be a new order in the world; and my sons would be right there in the thick of things! With their talent for management and their political savvy, I figured that James would very well end up as Secretary of State in Jesus' new kingdom, and John would be Diplomatic Representative to all the nations. It was only a matter of time.

As you know, most patient Father, I assumed that the promised Messiah would be political and powerful, blessed with military skill greater than King David's, displaying a majesty twice as splendid as Solomon's. We all thought that. It never dawned on of us that the Christ would be a victim soul, that he would be the fulfillment of the Suffering Servant who would take up the sins of all humankind and spell out, in his body, the anguish of the Man of Sorrows. Isaiah the prophet spoke of our savior in these terms (chapter 53).

(The prophet is amazed, as he proclaims:)
He seemed to us to be a leper,
one struck down by God and afflicted;
but he was bruised for our wickedness,
wounded for our sins.
the chastisements of our peace was put upon him;
and by his bruises, we are healed....
He had done no sin,
there was no deceit in his mouth
and yet the Lord laid on him
the injustices of us all!

(Then God responds:)
If he lay down his life for sin,
he shall save all people.
Because his soul has suffered
shall this, my Just Servant,
justify many and bear their sins.
Therefore, I will give him all peoples for his heritage,
and he shall destroy the power of the proud;
because he delivered himself up to death,
and was reputed with the wicked,

and has borne the sins of the many,
and has prayed for all transgressors.

None of us paid attention to this passage. We skipped over it, as well as all the psalms about the Afflicted One. We thought that these parts of our Scripture referred only to the many hardships our people endured through the centuries. We never connected such humiliations to our hopes for the Messiah.

Indeed, everyone was wrong about how the Promised One would reveal himself, once he got going. Oh, Jesus had power, all right, God-sent power. No doubt about that! But he wasn't using his power right! We were waiting for him to change, to finally become a leader who would topple the Roman Army of Occupation, crush the crippling tax collection system, and finally bring to justice the traitors who gave lip-service to Rome while keeping a strangle hold on their own people.

Jesus refused to use pressure or power. Each time he was pushed to be a king (the way we wanted him to be the king) he would run off to the mountains by himself. Then, one day, I thought up a ruse that maybe would get Jesus going. I asked that my two sons be placed in positions of power in the new kingdom he would soon set up. Of course, I was ambitious. I had designs on Herod's castle; and after the revolution, James and John would establish headquarters there. I would be the manager, the personal liaison between them and their staff.

Such were my thoughts, I admit. But more to the point, I wanted to find out (now that two years were already behind us) whether or not Jesus was ever going to be like Solomon in all his glory. Asking him to grant favors to my sons would force him to respond directly about what kind of government—if any—he was preparing for.

He didn't respond directly. As usual, his answer was evasive—he simply changed the subject. He brought up the theme of the Suffering Servant again! Then he warned the apostles not to play politics against each other. His kingdom would be one of service and patient love.

Well, that put me in my place! I prayed about the unsuccessful ultimatum I had delivered. I reflected (this time, with an open mind) about how consistent Jesus was in everything he said.

My ambition was good in itself. I wanted to heal the wounds of injustice for my people; I wanted peace to prosper and wars to end; I wanted taxes to be reasonable, and all laborers to get an honest wage for honest work. I wanted the whole world to be run as efficiently as I ran my home.

All well and good. But then I wanted to make everyone bend to my plan of peaceful enterprise. I was tempted the same way all ambitious people are. They start with high ideals and want their plans to work, but then they find that obstacles arise from laziness, or dullness of comprehension, or jealousy, or lack of cooperation because some people are too busy with their own priorities.

Then they get all wrapped up fighting for power, which can so consume them that they forget (as I did) things like love and peace, which their idealism began with. They then become schemers, sensitive to any favoritism that does not fit their plans. I had some of this drive in me.

Of course, as you know, Father, I wasn't all bad. In a short time, I came to my senses and modified my ways.

I guess I care so strongly for ambitious people that I get carried away for their causes. So many gifted people end in ruin, after they began so well. At first they show great promise, fine leadership skills, and magnetic personalities; they are motivated by the commendable desire to improve things for all. And then that drive for power turns ideals into factions, wars, and exploitation. Love has to be joined to their impulsiveness. The healing element of suffering has to find some place in their hearts. No good plan will ever bear fruit unless people are willing to suffer for it.

That's what the Lord told me. His compassion was a reprimand about my wrong use of power. Peter's mother-in-law was healed of her fever, then she began to wait on others. I had a fever, too, a different kind of fever: to do great things, and to have my children do great things. My magnanimity was a virtue, my pushiness was not.

I've gained much wisdom after Jesus led me to change. I have become more supple, better balanced, more pleasant to be around. Jesus accomplished all that I had hoped for, without my doing much about it. No, I was never appointed Lady Dowager of Herod's palace; James was never appointed Secretary of State. Tax collectors still gouge citizens around the world; peace has never been in force, never for long. The world still has its problems.

But the peace of Christ is always—for everyone—an inner possibility, and love still finds unique ways to serve others. And suffering makes sense, since it is linked to the passion, death and resurrection of our Lord.

Please, Good Father, let me use what I have learned, for the sake of ambitious people. The talent is there for them: and energy and trained efficiency. All they need is the balance that comes from compassion... and the readiness to suffer with enduring love.

Jesus Speaks

Yes, Father, it will do well for my cherished Thunder, mother of the "sons of thunder," to watch over those who are ambitious. She knows better than anyone how to get fruitful production from the most talented people. No one could be more qualified to counsel those who are especially driven to accomplish great things. She will help them to see the larger picture. By being compassionate, she will invest them with needed patience and a greater sense of "feeling with" those who work for them. She will be our mediator for pity. And once genuine pity is joined to the desire to do great things, the world will improve tremendously, managed by such a leadership of love.

God Speaks

So be it. With this, I think our session should adjourn. I only ask that James and John gather a sub-committee to devise ways to reach the children of ambitious people. These children suffer sometimes from their parents' pushiness. You felt this yourselves, Sons of Thunder, when you were growing up. But your drive was as great as your mother's, so it turned out well.

There are many others who are not so fortunate. Boys and girls are often pushed to excel in sports in order to please their parents.

But they perhaps would rather just run after butterflies. Many children get headaches that never leave them because they haven't achieved the success they were supposed to. They need our special care. They need to know that they are loveable even when they do not perform as brilliantly as they are expected to.

(God then turns toward the angels who have been transcribing the proceedings.)

Angelic secretaries, since you have transcribed the statements made by each of the volunteers—from the Mother at Cana to the Mother of James and John, please number them in order of appearance and code them according to their nicknames. Then distribute copies to everyone concerned.

The angelic secretaries, joined by all in heaven, say, "Amen."

The Grandmother

GOOD SAINT ANN

The Ancient legends provide us with details about the birth
and upbringing of the child of Ann and Joachim. She was
born in Jerusalem about the year 20 B.C. When Mary was
three years old, her parents brought her to the temple and
consecrated her to God. According to the Eastern legends,
she remained [for some years] as a ward of the priests. The
Western legends believe Mary returned home [soon] after
her presentation and continued her education from St. Ann.
  From "The Early Life of Mary," Holy Bible edited for the
Marian Year.

Near the cross of Jesus there stood his mother....Seeing his
mother there with the disciple whom he loved, Jesus said to
his mother, "Woman, there is your son."   John 19:25-26

The Grandmother Speaks
Please, my Lord, may I have the last word? In a sense, I am not a
gospel woman. I died long before the gospels were written down or
proclaimed. But, in a deeper sense, I do belong. I want to be the
instrument of your compassion for all who have not been included
in any other category. I want to be everybody's grandmother. No
matter how old people are, there is still the "little child" in their

hearts. And sometimes (especially when they are down) they'd like to cuddle in their grandmother's lap and hear good stories and learn that they can trust themselves because they are loved.

I want to be this person for them all, whenever they need me. I have a right to claim universal grandmother for myself. My grandson, with the very last words he said to any human, gave Mary to the world as mother. He called my daughter "woman," not "Mother." By this designation, he wanted everyone to know that she will always be *the* Woman—the New Eve—the one who, united to Jesus, would bring forth a brand new way of life for everyone. For me, too. In a sense, my daughter mothered me! Thanks to her and her son, I have been ushered into paradise where I live this new way of life with all of you.

Thank you, my daughter, for this most awesome event. I constantly marvel at the mystery. My own grandson mothered me! He brought me into the life of perfect happiness. So did you my daughter. By that adoption ceremony on Good Friday, I automatically became the grandmother of, and for, the world. And I accept. It will not be a duty, but a joy.

Here is a hint of how I will exercise this kind of compassion for all people. First, I want each of them to remember the best scene from their own childhood, when their grandparents cared for them: the very best times, the happiest delights, the loveliest memories they have. If they never had such experiences (because they never knew their grandparents, or for some other reason) I want them to imagine how it *could* have been, if only things had been different.

And that's what I will be for them. Any time, under any circumstances, when they want a good lap, a warm hug, an understanding and supportive older woman—who is family to them in the very best sense of the word—I will be there for them. All they need to do is ask.

Jesus Speaks
Yes, Grandmother, so be it. Thanks to you, we are certain that our compassion will reach everyone.

As you all know, I was one of those who never enjoyed the

happiness of a grandmother and grandfather. Ann died four years before I was born. Joachim, soon after. However, even though I never met you on earth, Ann, I always felt that I knew you. Mary told me so many stories about you. She would act them out and say, "When I was your age, son, and I'd come home from school with a scuffed knee, or a tear or two because somebody teased me, this is what my mother would do." And Mary would do the same for me. So I felt as though both mothers were loving me and caring for me at the same time.

It was so good. I was so blessed and I am forever grateful.

One thing more, Father, before we end our session. I ask my grandmother to show special concern for all those older people—of grandparent age—who are afflicted with self-doubts. I was so afflicted in the Garden of Gethsemane. I wasn't old, of course, but I felt old, knowing I would die the next day. Part of my agony was wondering if my life meant anything to anybody. Would my teaching and example have any lasting effect? Would my disciples catch my spirit and continue? Or would they just run away, take up their former occupations, and forget me? Would the people I healed and preached to remember how I loved them. Or did I live my life in vain?

I didn't know. I wasn't sure. That was the excruciating pain of it. I just hoped that my life really could be considered worthwhile.

When I arrived here in heaven, I shared all this with Good Saint Ann, who admitted that she had feelings somewhat similar to mine, when she was dying.

She thought she did her best, as wife and mother. She hoped she did, but how could anyone know for certain? Her life went past her, and nothing could be done to bring it back. All she could do was trust God that things would be all right in the future, that Mary would grow up well and make her proud. She didn't know how it would turn out; like every other person, she had to hope....

At the time of leave-taking, everyone has these doubts. Life isn't like a report card at the end of a school year. Nobody has guarantees that their life has been a success, that their deeds and words would live well after them. All humans have self-doubts on these occasions. Some even experience terrible anxieties about it. I want Ann to be with them especially. She will put their fears upon her lap. She will help them to be children once again—to trust in the feeling of her abiding love, to hope in the future, because God (who *is* compassion) embraces their future.

Saint Ann will ease them into a place of peace where she will soothe their fears and tell them stories to distract them from depression. And she will end with the greatest story of them all:

> How their mother Mary and their grandmother Ann
> join with me
> to bring them into a brand new way of life
> where all good wishes really do come true
> in the place—the only place—
> where there is "living ever after, happily."

God Concludes

So be it. It is decided. Good Saint Ann, you are the grandmother of the world. You reach those who are unreachable in any other way.

Compassion was the first word as we began. Let it be our last. So be it. No need for a response this time. The response must come from those on earth who are willing to accept our love. Amen.

Additional Titles by Father Isaias Powers, C.P.

Letters from an Understanding Friend

A creative way to reflect and meditate on the message of the Gospel, with inspiring letters from Jesus.
ISBN: 0-89622-413-9, 96 pp, $5.95

Audiobook: Three 60-minute cassettes, $24.95

Quiet Places with Jesus

Each meditation in this guided imagery primer begins with a Scripture quotation, followed by a reflection, and then a poetic invitation into prayer.
ISBN: 0-89622-086-9, 128 pp, $5.95

Audiobook: Three 60-minute cassettes, $24.95

Quiet Places with Mary

24 guided imagery meditations are directed to living life in the image of God, as revealed by Jesus, with Mary as a companion.
ISBN: 0-89622-297-7, 160 pp, $5.95

Audiobook: Three 60-minute cassettes, $24.95

A Personal Way of the Cross

14 meditations and an opening prayer pinpoint direct links between Jesus' experiences of suffering and those lived by everyone today.
ISBN: 0-89622-319-1, 32 pp, 99¢

VIDEO

On Retreat With Father Ike

Each of the six parts of this video series opens with Father Powers leading the viewer in prayer. He effectively makes connections between Jesus' words and viewers' lives. Each segment closes with a suggestion for group discussion and personal prayer.
Six 15-20-minute videos, $149.00

Available at religious bookstores or from
TWENTY-THIRD PUBLICATIONS
P.O. Box 180 • Mystic, CT 06355 • **1-800-321-0411**